The Thinki

OLGA MCIVOR

The Thinking Processes Curriculum

A book for teachers, administrators, and curriculum developers

VDM Verlag Dr. Müller

Impressum/Imprint (nur für Deutschland/ only for Germany)
Bibliografische Information der Deutschen Nationalbibliothek: Die Deutsche Nationalbibliothek
verzeichnet diese Publikation in der Deutschen Nationalbibliografie; detaillierte bibliografische
Daten sind im Internet über http://dnb.d-nb.de abrufbar.
 Alle in diesem Buch genannten Marken und Produktnamen unterliegen warenzeichen-, marken-
oder patentrechtlichem Schutz bzw. sind Warenzeichen oder eingetragene Warenzeichen der
jeweiligen Inhaber. Die Wiedergabe von Marken, Produktnamen, Gebrauchsnamen,
Handelsnamen, Warenbezeichnungen u.s.w. in diesem Werk berechtigt auch ohne besondere
Kennzeichnung nicht zu der Annahme, dass solche Namen im Sinne der Warenzeichen- und
Markenschutzgesetzgebung als frei zu betrachten wären und daher von jedermann benutzt
werden dürften.

Coverbild: www.ingimage.com

Verlag: VDM Verlag Dr. Müller GmbH & Co. KG
Dudweiler Landstr. 99, 66123 Saarbrücken, Deutschland
Telefon +49 681 9100-698, Telefax +49 681 9100-988
Email: info@vdm-verlag.de

Herstellung in Deutschland:
Schaltungsdienst Lange o.H.G., Berlin
Books on Demand GmbH, Norderstedt
Reha GmbH, Saarbrücken
Amazon Distribution GmbH, Leipzig
ISBN: 978-3-639-36288-6

Imprint (only for USA, GB)
Bibliographic information published by the Deutsche Nationalbibliothek: The Deutsche
Nationalbibliothek lists this publication in the Deutsche Nationalbibliografie; detailed
bibliographic data are available in the Internet at http://dnb.d-nb.de.
 Any brand names and product names mentioned in this book are subject to trademark, brand
or patent protection and are trademarks or registered trademarks of their respective holders. The
use of brand names, product names, common names, trade names, product descriptions etc.
even without a particular marking in this works is in no way to be construed to mean that such
names may be regarded as unrestricted in respect of trademark and brand protection legislation
and could thus be used by anyone.

Cover image: www.ingimage.com

Publisher: VDM Verlag Dr. Müller GmbH & Co. KG
Dudweiler Landstr. 99, 66123 Saarbrücken, Germany
Phone +49 681 9100-698, Fax +49 681 9100-988
Email: info@vdm-publishing.com

Printed in the U.S.A.
Printed in the U.K. by (see last page)
ISBN: 978-3-639-36288-6

Acknowledgements

I would like to thank Dr. Arnold Novak, Chairman of Graduate Studies, Brandon University, Brandon, Manitoba, for his guidance and assistance in the selection of my graduate courses.

I wish to thank Dr. K. P. Binda for compelling me to answer questions that required a lot of reading on curriculum material. Reading all the material has given me the tools to effectively organize and develop curricula.

I also wish to thank Dr. Thomas MacNeill for agreeing to be my advisor. He provided me with direction, assistance, and guidance in developing my curriculum project. His recommendations and suggestions have been invaluable for the improvement of my project.

Special thanks to Dr. Marion Terry for agreeing to be my reader. She helped me clean up my words and kept me honest when I drifted off course. She was very patient and meticulous in editing my work.

Sincere thanks to my friend and colleague, Dr. Irene Huggins for encouraging me and supporting me to complete my project. She persuaded me to keep working on the project even when I thought I didn't have time for it during our hectic travel schedules at work.

TABLE OF CONTENTS

INTRODUCTION

The world demands that students become effective and skillful thinkers. There has been a tremendous increase in knowledge in the last half-century. Educational institutions need to acknowledge this phenomenon, which is due to the collective influence of the growth of technology, and the steady transition from an industrial to an information society (Toffler, 1990, p. 9). There have been many changes in education, and it continues to change as educators and concerned citizens try to make sense of reality and how education should function within it. The volume of available information has become overwhelming due to technology; so knowledge alone can no longer serve as a criterion for being educated (Wiles & Bondi, 2007, p. 30). The diversities and complexities of society bring different ideas of the nature and purpose of education within society which has an impact on curricula in school and how they are taught (Ornstein & Hunkins, 2004, p. 167). There is a paradigm shift in education to accommodate the age of technology and information, and Wiles and Bondi (2007 p. 33) believe that this shift will redefine education and learning. To accommodate this paradigm in education, Fullan (2007) suggests that reculturing and questioning pedagogical assumptions or a shift of beliefs is necessary (p. 30). The content of a thinking curriculum include the various processes involved in decision making, creative thinking, critical thinking, problem solving, and metacognition. The following literature review highlights the necessity of preparing students for the information-intensive, fast-changing, and complex world of tomorrow.

There has been a knowledge explosion as well as in its accessibility, due to the growth of technology and the

3

internet. The economy is taking on a new structure that is fast-changing, diverse, and complex (Toffler, 1990, p. 72). As a result on these changes, society requires a radically higher level of knowledge processing and mind work. Toffler posits that high speed change requires high speed decisions. De Bono (1976) posits that the human mind cannot absorb an exponential amount of data; so it is the application of thinking to the data that will make sense of it and generate ideas (p. 34). De Bono believes that as we collect information, we are collecting data that has been organized by our ideas, so we need to think to improve on those ideas. Walker and Antaya-Moore (1999) claim that students have to organize this information, find patterns in it, and try to make sense of all the information (p. 2). These authors assert that simply knowing things is not enough, and that society expects more out of schools. Schools are expected to prepare students to communicate effectively, work in teams, analyze and solve problems, reflect on their learning, and develop new ideas. An individual should be proficient in the thinking skills and thinking processes in order to interpret, analyze, and evaluate the vast amount of information (Victorian Curriculum and Assessment Authority [VCAA], 2008, p. 77).

A thinking curriculum for any school must acknowledge the diversities of the student population. De Bono (1976) defines thinking as "exploring of experience for a purpose" (p. 82). He believes the purpose of thinking is to clarify perceptions and the processing of information for use. Students come to classrooms with varied experiences and knowledge because of their life experiences and backgrounds. People have experiences with each other, and start to construct knowledge as they develop

4

understandings about what those experiences mean (Thayer-Bacon, 2000, p. 2). Essentially, people, ideas, and experiences are connected and interconnected. In our extremely interconnected and interdependent world, students have to learn to work with others by building positive social relationships, and by working and learning in teams (VCAA, 2008, p. 8). Knowledge is validated by thinking and allows individuals to construct new knowledge, build ideas, and make connections between them (VCAA, 2008, p. 77). When students are actively engaged in the construction of their own learning and meaning, they will be inspired to go further in their learning (Fullan, 2007, p. 187).

As society changes, traditional pedagogic approaches are not always suited to current learning environments. Saskatchewan Education (1987) indicates that the role of the educator is to help the student develop and refine thinking abilities (p. 5). This process includes being able to provide the classroom climate and teaching practices that can best support thinking skills. The levels of pedagogic knowledge are changing and schools find themselves in a society that is evolving (Ornstein and Hunkins, 2004, p. 213). Ornstein and Hunkins reminds us of the relatively slow speed of the change process, as individuals need time to learn new skills, and formulate new attitudes (p. 315). Fullan (2007) explains that this restructuring may require reculturing, whereby teachers are required to question, and change their beliefs and habits for the improvement of teaching and learning (p. 25). While change may take time, students need to develop robust thinking skills now in order to ensure that they can be productive and fulfilled participants throughout their lives.

5

The purpose of a thinking curriculum is to develop productive habits of mind that will facilitate learning for the students. The content of the curriculum is encompassed in the thinking processes involved in the strands. The contexts in which these habits of mind will be developed are included in the outcomes and achievement indicators. Productive habits of mind will help students resist manipulation, and form rational points of view about their own thinking and the thinking of other people. VCAA (2008) claims that this transformation is possible if students are given sufficient time to think and reflect in a school environment that promotes and encourages thinking in the classroom (p. 77).

THINKING PROCESSES FRAMEWORK

This curriculum framework is comprised of thinking skills and thinking processes. De Bono (1976) recommends that a thinking program should have a definite structure and form (p. 25). The general and specific outcomes, as well as the achievement indicators make up the explicit structure and form in this curriculum. Marzano and Arredondo (1986) argue that schools should be restructured in order to effectively educate youth to live successfully in the information age (p. 25). The development of thinking can be supported in schools by implementing a specific program, curricular materials, and pedagogic development (McGregor, 2007, p. 313).

The curriculum framework identifies the outcomes that students are expected to know and be able to achieve through the processes of decision making, creative thinking, critical thinking, problem solving, and metacognition. The processes of thinking include

6

reasoning and making connections. Reasoning is the logical thinking that help us to solve problems and determine if and why our responses make sense. Making connections within and among ideas is the key to learning. The curriculum framework provides the context of learning in the outcomes and achievement indicators. The habits of mind are at the heart of the curriculum and require students to be active participants in the learning process. Integrating the heads and hearts of learners will create independent thinkers and life-long learners. The purpose of this document is to provide direction to educators in preparing students for a world of information intensive, fast-changing culture.

The Thinking Processes Framework consists of the following: introduction, rationale, and purpose of framework; goals for students and teachers; overview and explanation of the strands ; general outcomes, specific outcomes, and achievement indicators; discussion of the learning   environment,   suggestions   for   pedagogical approaches, recommended resources, and a sample lesson plan.

> "The heart of the educational enterprise takes place within the learner. For all learners, there are 2 fundamental motivators that bring about learning. They are necessity and curiosity. When it is not necessary to do so, individuals do very little thinking. This is especially true when one's habit patterns are sufficient to take care of the individual satisfactorily. Thinking begins when habits fail."
>
> (Lowery, 1996, p. 3)

Rationale

The rationale of developing a thinking curriculum is to prepare and support students in becoming effective and skillful thinkers. Students are curious, active learners with individual interests, abilities, and needs (K-4 Math, 1995, p. 4). They come to classrooms with varying knowledge, life experiences, and backgrounds. A key element is to make connections to those backgrounds and experiences, in order to develop thinking skills and thinking processes. From a pragmatic perspective, thinking is based on a view that people's experiences are not separate from their perceptions and ideas; therefore, reality is actually experienced (Wiles and Bondi, 2007, p. 44). Social constructivism and relational ontology and epistemology start with the assumption that people have experiences with each other and develop ideas and understandings about what those experiences mean, and they begin to construct knowledge (Thayer-Bacon, 2000, p. 3). Constructivism places the individual as an active participant in the process of thinking, learning, and coming to know (Ornstein and Hunkins, 2004, p. 117). Students have to discuss understandings or misunderstandings. VCAA (2008) maintains that thinking validates knowledge and facilitates the creation of new knowledge (p. 5). Learning should be done in a meaningful context where students' experiences and backgrounds are acknowledged and valued (Manitoba Education, Citizenship and Youth [MECY], 2003, p. 5). Students need to be respected and accepted as an important aspect of the learning environment. Ornstein and Hunkins (2004) argue that educators have to be selective in determining and organizing the experiences of the learners, in order to improve society (p. 135).

8

In this information age, Wiles and Bondi (2007) believe that educators need to support students in developing their thinking skills in order to prepare them for a paradigm shift in society (p. 307). They maintain that work in the future will be a "head" function and knowledge will have more value in its application than just acquisition (p. 307). The workers of tomorrow will need to make important decisions without delay and under pressure. To function effectively tomorrow, students have to analyze what they are learning today by applying reasoning processes that will help them extend and refine information. Developing productive habits of mind is essential for successful learning. Education should facilitate self-understanding and help children develop the disposition to be open-minded so that they will not just passively accept the status quo but become independent thinkers (Kite, 2000, p. 13). Kite posits that independent thinkers will be able to resist manipulation, and form rational points of view about their own thinking, and the thinking of others. VCAA (2008) purport that this is possible if the school environment promotes thinking in the classroom (p. 5).

GOALS FOR STUDENTS AND EDUCATORS

Educators need to prepare and support students as they develop proficiency in decision making, critical thinking, creative thinking, problem solving, and metacognitive thinking (i.e., thinking about what they are thinking). Educators have to support, encourage, and challenge students to develop their own learning practices. Kite (2000) asserts that students must be given opportunities to plan their thinking in order to have the confidence to take cognitive risks and realize that problems may be difficult but not impossible to solve (p. 9). Kite believes that the goal for students involves developing individuals who value knowledge and learning, and who can and will think for themselves. Kite further suggests that students be challenged to make meaning by critical reflection, questioning, and consideration of others' points of view. Wilks (2005) contends that the students' role is to think, inquire, discuss, and figure out the best responses to problems and issues (p. 31).

Educators must be role models for learning when they step into a classroom. According to Walker and Antaya-Moore (1999), teachers have an extraordinary power to influence students; so they have to be passionate about learning (p. xii). Educators have to be problem solvers, learners and effective thinkers. Educators must create an active, reflective learning environment wherein students can have a personal interest in what they are learning. According to Wilks (2005), the teacher's main role is to be a facilitator and coach for students so they can develop thinking skills and behaviors (p. 53). McGregor (2007) posits that educators have countless opportunities to structure children's learning blueprint and thinking for life (p. 1). Teachers must be willing to learn along with their students. McGregor also maintains that schools are places of growth for children, teachers, and administrators; so the pursuit of intellectual activity and professional collaboration should be encouraged and supported (p. 303).

The workers of tomorrow will need to think and be capable of making decisions quickly, despite the soaring load of available information (Toffler, 1990, p. 206). Toffler claims that students will need to have a good attitude, as there will be a continuous cycle of learning, unlearning, and relearning of new techniques in different organizational forms. Toffler discusses a fast-changing environment, wherein rules will be changed and individuals will need to adapt and be able to come up with new ideas (p. 207). Wiles and Bondi (2007) suggest that individuals should have various thinking skills, collaboration skills, and an entrepreneurial spirit (p. 307). Integrating the heads and hearts of students will make them independent thinkers and life-long learners.

General Student Learning Outcomes

General student learning outcomes are overarching statements identifying what students are expected to learn in each strand. The general outcome for each strand is the same or very similar throughout the grades.

Specific Student Learning Outcomes

Specific student learning outcomes are statements identifying the component knowledge, skills, and attitudes of a general outcome.

Achievement Indicators
Achievement Indicators are sets of indicators that are used to determine whether students have met the target for the corresponding specific outcome. The achievement indicators show the depth, breadth, and expectations for students in their learning.

Summary

The framework for K-12 thinking processes describes the skills and processes to be addressed in this K-12 thinking processes curriculum. Five strands have been identified for Kindergarten to Grade 12 to reinforce the interrelationships of thinking skills and thinking processes. The processes of thinking include reasoning and making connections. Reasoning is the logical thinking that help us to solve problems and determine if and why our responses make sense. Making connections within and among ideas is the key to learning. The thinking processes involved include decision making, creative thinking, critical thinking, problem solving and metacognition. The thinking processes of the curriculum is the content that students are expected to learn and live by. The strands are the formal aspect of the discipline of thinking processes. The strands form the foundation of the Framework and act as links across the grade levels. The thinking skills include the student outcomes that are organized under the five strands. The thinking skills are the habits of mind that have to be explicitly taught and reinforced.

There is no chronological order for using the strands. Educators can start with any strand and proceed with any other strand. Discussion of historical and current issues and events is recommended for using the Thinking Processes curriculum. The outcomes are developed and based on the expectation that they are appropriate for the general majority of students. They appear at the grade level where they are expected to be "mastered." There may be some delays between the time that the students first meet the learning outcome and when they are expected to demonstrate mastery of the skill.

The Strands of Decision Making, Creative Thinking, Critical Thinking, Problem Solving, and Metacognition are described in the following pages.

"Understanding is a measure of the quality and quantity of connections that a new idea has with existing ideas. The greater the number of connections to a network of ideas, the better the understanding."
(Van de Walle & Lovin, 2006, p. 3)

1. Decision Making Strand

The process of decision making involves recognizing a problem or challenge in a situation, identifying and evaluating alternatives, and then acting on the best alternative. Action is required in making a decision; it is not just a mental process. A decision, by itself, is a firm mental resolution about future action. Society has placed more emphasis on the cognitive aspect of decision making and not enough on the action required to implement a decision. Decisions need action. Decision making is an important process and should not be taken lightly. De Bono further claims that our values, feelings, and emotions determine the kind of decision to act upon (p. 99).

BCMH (1983) indicates that decision making is based on some assumptions, and that learning to think for oneself requires an understanding of external influences, such as peer pressure and advertising (p. 4). There are also internal influences that include one's values and beliefs, which impact on the kind of decisions made. BCMH claim that the inability to think independently contributes largely to the social acceptance of alcohol and drug use (p. 6). When students decide on the best course of action, after deliberating on why it should be done, and whether it is right or wrong, it will elucidate their values (Kite, 2000, p. 14). Kite (2000) posits that when students make decisions about real life issues that affect them, it will help them see that they are responsible for the decisions they make (p. 14).

Martin (2003) maintains that our view of reality (ontology) influences how we develop an awareness of others and ourselves (pp. 6-9). Our view of reality helps in getting to know our responsibilities and ways to relate to self and to others. According to Martin, our ways of knowing have to do with how this ontology is learned and replicated through listening, sensing, exchanging, sharing, engaging, and applying. Ontology is impacted by social, political, historical and spatial dimensions of individuals, and the group and interactions with outsiders. Thayer-Bacon (2000) believes that our ideas come from our experiences and transactions with others (p. 7). This author also says that a socially constructed view of knowledge is something that is constantly reconstructed and deconstructed with the help of other people. Interaction with people is an essential part of living, learning, and making good decisions. The educational system must acknowledge that students come to school with different worldviews and have different knowledge and realities that are vital to their continued existence. Students will learn how to learn when they are actively participating, and thinking skills will then become an integral part of their studies (MET, 1996, p. 8).

"Decisions not only have to be made but they also have to be acted upon."
(De Bono, 1983, p. 112).

2. Creative Thinking Strand

Creative thinking is the establishment of new approaches to a problem or an alternative point of view. Creative thinking is concerned with generating something new (McGregor, 2007, p. 169). The capacity to think creatively is a central component of being able to solve problems and being innovative (VCAA, 2008, p. 78). Creative thinking enables students to make observations and decisions to solve problems and to devise forward-thinking strategies (MECY, 2003, p. 15). MECY states that creative thinking

- emphasizes divergent thinking that promotes the generation of ideas and possibilities, and

- helps in the exploration of diverse approaches to questions (p. 15).

Creative thinking happens when students identify unique connections among ideas and suggest insightful approaches to questions and issues (Alberta Education, 2005, p. 8). Alberta Education states that through creative thinking, students generate an inventory of possibilities; anticipate outcomes; and combine logical, intuitive and divergent thought. Creative thinking is a process of inquiry, analysis, and evaluation, which results in a reasoned judgment.

Pedagogic approaches that support creative thinking provide open-ended tasks, challenges, problems or issues to be acted upon or thought about (McGregor, 2007, p. 187). McGregor thinks that students should be encouraged to personalize connections and transfer the thinking from a school context to real-life situations. More importantly, in creative thinking, there is no one fixed "right" answer, so students might have fun exploring ideas.

De Bono (1983) claims that humour is the most significant characteristic of the human mind, but people pay little attention to it (p. 57). He contends that humour can go from one pattern and switch to another pattern, such as the double meaning in a pun type of humour. Another mechanism of humour is being taken to an unreasonable point and suddenly going back, such as punch lines that use alternative perceptions of familiar situations (De Bono, p. 57). Humour increases the ability for flexible thinking and finding creative solutions to problems (Kite, 2000, p. 16). Kite maintains that using humour to stimulate creative thinking is now widely recognized; humour liberates creativity and promotes higher-order thinking (p. 16).

"Creative thinking requires open questions to encourage it; often requires longer 'incubation' or cogitating time; often slower/longer to nurture; and is more contemplative in nature."
(McGregor, 2007, p. 186)

3. Critical Thinking Strand

Critical thinking is an examination and judgment of an idea while looking for clarity and accuracy. Thinking is often casual or routine, but critical thinking evaluates the quality of thinking. According to Thayer-Bacon (2000), critical thinking is a "specialized form of thinking" used to make judgments about "good" answers, offer justifications, and review arguments (p. 127). Thayer-Bacon further states that critical thinkers should focus on questions and use logical induction and deduction to select the best responses (p. 128). Inductive reasoning moves from specific observations to detecting patterns and regularities, finally ending up with general conclusions. MECY (2008b) defines induction as deriving general conclusions from specific observations or situations (p. 13). Deductive reasoning works from the more general to the more specific. Ornstein and Hunkins (2004) define deductive reasoning as the process of using general statements to come to conclusions about specific information or situations (p. 176).

According to Dewey, "what we believe influences what we think and we base our beliefs on evidence we have evaluated" as cited in McGregor (2007, p. 191). Our worldviews and experiences are the basis of how we see reality and the world (Wilson, 2001, p. 176). Wilson further maintains that how we think about reality determines how we are going to use our ways of thinking to gain more knowledge about that reality (p. 175). Our realities are different from other people and we see things through different lenses. Thayer-Bacon (2000) contends that critical thinking is embedded within a context of lived experiences and is open to the possibilities of biases (p. 34). Even when we try to be objective, our actions are ruled by our beliefs. Kite (2000) maintains that the main concern of critical thinking is deciding what we should believe and what we should do (p. 13). Kite suggests that education should facilitate self-understanding and help children develop the disposition to be open-minded so that they will not just passively accept the status quo but become independent thinkers. Independent thinkers should be able to resist manipulation, and form rational points of view about their own thinking and the thinking of others (BCMH, 1983, p. 6).

McGregor (2007) explains that critical thinking often requires more focused questions to encourage an examination and judgment of something (p. 186). There is often only one correct outcome and it requires reflection on the matter to be considered or critiqued. Critical thinking is a tool to help us solve problems and make decisions.

> *"Questioning in a live and "learning" mind never ends. Questions become transformed. Questions generate more questions. Questions stimulate new ways to think, and make new paths to follow as we analyze, and evaluate thinking. Questions improve our thinking."*
> *(Elder and Paul, 2006, p. 4)*

4. Problem Solving Strand

Problem solving is engaging in a task for which the solution is not obvious or known in advance. McGregor (2007) argues that learners engaged in open-ended problem solving tasks can develop useful, wide-ranging thinking (p. 65). Social constructivism supports and encourages collaborating students to resolve problems by sharing and reflecting ideas (Ibid., 2007, p. 65). Students should have opportunities to solve problems that affect their own lives and experience the consequences of their decisions. Kite (2000) maintains that students can learn to appreciate that they have control over their lives and learning when they deal with real-life problems (p. 9). Problem solving skills can be developed by being open to listening, discussing, and trying different strategies. Problem solving requires students to use prior knowledge in new ways and in new contexts. Van de Walle and Folk (2005) hold that problem solving places the focus of the students' attention on ideas and sense making (p. 44). Solving problems offers potential for nurturing thinking skills if problems are drawn collectively in small groups (McGregor 2007, p. 44). McGregor also maintains that the problems should be connected to life out of school and life after school.

Research indicates that children's performance is strongly influenced by their beliefs regarding the extent to which they control and have the capability to succeed (Kite, 2000, p. 15). Kite maintains that when students have poor self-concepts, they are unlikely to succeed at their task. A positive self-concept is an important factor in successful learning and must be nurtured in all students. Thayer-Bacon (2007) states that knowledge and knowers are

20

interconnected and interrelated (p. 3), therefore, learning is a social affair (p. 132). Ideas are not separate from experiences and there is a connection between thinking and doing (p. 38). The level at which learning and thinking tasks can be posed and presented is supported by social constructivism (McGregor, 2007, p. 65).

A thinking processes curriculum and especially problem solving has to embrace feelings, attitudes, beliefs and values (Kite, 2000, p. 9). Educators must realize and acknowledge that students come to school with different worldviews and different experiences, and diversity has to be supported and respected in the classroom.

"Problem solving provides ongoing assessment data that can be used to make instructional decisions, help students succeed, and inform parents."
(Van de Walle & Folk, 2005, p. 44)

5. Metacognition Strand

Metacognition is "thinking about thinking" (Alberta Learning, 2005, p. 9). It involves critical self-awareness, conscious reflection, analysis, monitoring, and reinvention. Students assess the value of the learning strategies that they have used, modify them or select new strategies, and monitor the use of reinvented or new strategies in future learning situations. In this respect, students become knowledge creators and contribute to a shared understanding of the world we live in. Alberta Learning (2005) maintains that metacognition encompasses all the thinking that we do to evaluate our own mental processes and to plan for appropriate use of these processes in order to meet the demands of the situation (p. 9).

Building an environment for thinking will mean recognizing, supporting, and teaching the role of metacognition. Metacognition is about reflecting on cognitive processes and strategies used during a learning experience (McGregor, 2007, p. 228). Alberta Learning (2005) indicates that metacognitive skills are part of the "learning to learn" skills that are transferable to new learning situations, in and out of school (p. 2). Understanding and learning to deal with thoughts and feelings are good learning experiences for students and teachers.

22

The absence of threat is an absolute prerequisite for reaching the mental state of reflective thinking (Kovalik & Olsen, 2005, p. 2.11). A safe environment is a place, where students can take risks, and even fail, and learn from their mistakes (Thayer-Bacon, 2000, p. 133). Students should recognize and appreciate that making mistakes is part of learning. Reflection of ideas in the classroom should be shared with other students, in order for them to appreciate other people's point of view. Students who are comfortable sharing their ideas and alternative approaches will be better risk takers. MECY (2008a) maintains that when students develop metacognitive skills, they are able to adjust what they are doing and are able to improve the quality of their work (p. 13). As students expand their metacognitive skills, they will learn to be less dependent on the teacher and should be capable of independently monitoring the quality of their work. A pragmatic approach views knowledge as something that is socially constructed by people in relation with each other (Thayer-Bacon, 2000, p. 2). Ideas change and knowledge expands as people interact with each other and their experiences (p. 13).

"The ability and the inclination to think reflectively is an invaluable habit of mind. It lowers stress and improves learning and decision making."
(Kovalik & Olsen, 2005, p. 2.11)

INSTRUCTIONAL FOCUS

Society is changing, and traditional pedagogic approaches are not always suited to current learning environments. Today, the authority of the teacher should focus on being the one who knows how to foster deep understanding of big ideas and powerful processes, instead of being the "one who knows" (Wilks, 2005, p. 123). McGregor (2007) states that supporting thinking requires a range of pedagogic approaches that contrast with the present transmission teaching or direct instruction (p. 275). Wilks (2005) maintains that teachers will have to go beyond skill-based education to concept-driven design education (p. 130). Concept-based projects will not lend themselves to precise quantified or analytical grading, but rather to holistic grading (Wilks, 2005, p. 130). Teachers will have to be facilitators and coaches in order to help students develop thinking skills and behaviors. Walsh (2007) believes that teachers who model effective thinking strategies can help students do the same (p. 14). Fullan (2007) suggests that educators need a deep theoretical understanding of the principles and theories of pedagogy before making changes (301).

A social constructivist paradigm supports spontaneous development of thinking processes through interaction in a variety of learning activities (McGregor, 2007, p. 640). To effectively use thinking classrooms, educators should recognize when appropriate opportunities exist and how to nurture different kinds of thinking in the learning situations (McGregor, p. 64). Van de Walle and Folk (2005) hold that learning occurs best when it is acquired in a meaningful context, when it is based on students' existing knowledge, and when students are given opportunities to communicate their thinking (p. 29). They contend that children construct their own knowledge (p. 30). De Bono (1976) noted that poor verbal skills do not equate to poor thinking skills (p. 36). Educators have to be cognizant of diverse learning needs, such as learning disabilities or students with English as a second language. Wait time or processing time is required in order for students to digest information and respond. Learning should be done in a meaningful context when students' experiences and backgrounds are acknowledged and valued, according to MECY, (2003, p. 5).

MECY (2003) recommends that the following strategies be used in discovery learning: cooperative and peer learning, interviews, project-based learning, structured controversy or debate, teacher and student initiated inquiry and research, role play, and sharing circles (p. 5). Kite (2000) suggests using humour in the classroom for promoting flexible thinking and creative thinking (p. 16). Alberta Learning (2004) recommends that educators pose questions about thinking and feeling, and allow students to reflect upon their learning process, model the inquiry process out loud on a consistent basis, and review the inquiry process through class discussions, journal writing, and ongoing analyses of the data generated (p. 2).

BUILDING AN ENVIRONMENT FOR THINKING

Students need to acquire not only the skills and techniques for effective thinking, but also the concepts and habits that will allow them to become more aware and gain more control of their own behaviors as thinkers and problem solvers. Creating dispositions for good thinking has much to do with developing better thinking and reasoning skills (McGuinness, 1999, para 2). McGuinness suggests that teachers need to have open-minded attitudes about the nature of knowledge and thinking in order to create an educational atmosphere where talking about thinking – questioning, predicting, contradicting, doubting – is not only tolerated but actively pursued (para 15). An environment for teaching thinking will necessitate consideration of real problems and real solutions so that students can make decisions that affect their lives (Kite, 2000, p. 9). Kite suggests that educators have to acknowledge that feelings, attitudes, beliefs, and values are involved in teaching thinking. Understanding and learning to deal with thoughts and feelings makes a good learning experience for students and teachers. Students who are comfortable sharing their ideas and alternative approaches will be better risk takers.

Students should recognize and appreciate that making mistakes are part of learning. Kite suggests that if students are to take charge and control their own thinking, they should have opportunities to plan their thinking (p. 14). Involving students in constructing their own learning and meaning is essential so they can be motivated to do more (Fullan, 2007, p. 187). Fullan encourages educators to engage the students in the introduction and implementation of reform in the schools as active participants of change (p. 170). Education will be successful if the hearts and minds of students are engaged (p. 171).

There should be more time for thinking and reflecting, and less time on the reproduction and gathering of facts and information (Wilks, 2005, p. 99). The author posits that students should discuss their points of view and demonstrate that they can be engaged in meaningful inquiry and analysis (p. 99). She also suggests that the questions and ideas that are explored should be from the interests of the students. Wilks recommends activities that require students to demonstrate their ability to analyze, synthesize, and evaluate, in order for them to improve their thinking.

"Fear limits exploration. Threat, real or perceived, significantly restricts, if not eliminates, students' ability to fully engage in the learning process. To explore the new and different and to be open to new ideas requires confidence that one is in a safe environment, one in which mistakes and difficulty in understanding/doing something are considered just part of learning, not an opportunity for sarcasm and put-downs."
(Kovalik & Olsen, 2005, p. 1.27)

CODING SYSTEM FOR STUDENT LEARNING OUTCOMES

A coding system, shown in the chart below, has been developed for ease in locating learning outcomes and grade levels within a strand in the document.

CODING SYSTEM FOR OUTCOMES		
PS.A.3		
The **first letter** identifies the strand and the strands are:	The **second letter** identifies the grade level. Letters vary to reflect the three different levels.	The **Arabic numeral** identifies the specific learning outcome within a strand.
DM – Decision Making		
C – Creative Thinking	**Level A – Kindergarten to grade four**	The specific learning outcomes fall under each general outcome.
CRIT – Critical Thinking	**Level B – Grades five to eight**	Approximately 10-12 specific outcomes.
PS – Problem Solving	**Level C – Grades nine to twelve**	
M - Metacognition		

STUDENT LEARNING OUTCOMES

This section presents the general and specific outcomes for each strand for Kindergarten to Grade 12.

The general and specific learning outcomes contained in the strands are organized by grade level groupings:

Level A - Kindergarten to grade four (K-4);

Level B - Grades five to eight (5-8); and

Level C - Grades nine to twelve (9-12).

Group K-4 may not have as many specific outcomes as the higher grade grouping due to maturation levels of the students.

The list of specific outcomes contained in the document is not intended to be exhaustive but rather to provide teachers with examples of evidence of understanding that may be used in determining whether or not students understand a given outcome.

Teachers may use any number of specific outcomes, or they may choose to use other indicators as evidence that the desired learning has been achieved. Specific learning outcomes with the achievement indicators should help teachers form a clear picture of the intent and scope of each thinking outcome.

29

STRANDS AND GENERAL OUTCOMES

The thinking framework outlines the general outcomes within the five strands. The five strands serve as the foundation for the thinking framework. The content of the curriculum include the thinking processes involved in the strands. The strands (in their grade levels) can be used in any order; there is no hierarchy or prerequisite. The thinking skills are the habits of mind that have to be developed through the context of these outcomes. Each outcome is achieved through communication, listening, thinking, and reflecting on learning experiences. The general outcomes containing specific learning outcomes categorized under the headings start on page 32.

Decision Making (DM)
Identify the Problem
Identify the Alternatives
Evaluate Alternatives
Act on the Best Alternative

Creative Thinking (C)
Exhibit Curiosity
Explore New Ideas
Develop Flexibility

Critical Thinking (CRIT)
General Inquiry
Develop Inductive Thinking
Develop Deductive Thinking

Problem Solving   (PS)
Find and Define the Problem
Generate Alternative Solutions

Select and Implement a Plan
Evaluate results

Metacognition (M)

Develop Self-awareness
Review and Make Improvements
Promote Time Management
Refine Reflection Skills

THE STRANDS, GENERAL OUTCOMES, AND SPECIFIC LEARNING OUTCOMES WITHIN THE GRADE LEVELS ARE IN THE FOLLOWING BOXES.

STRANDS, GENERAL OUTCOMES AND SPECIFIC OUTCOMES	LEVEL A - K-4 LEVEL B - GRADES 5-8 LEVEL C - GRADES 9-12
DECISION MAKING	32-35
CREATIVE THINKING	36-38
CRITICAL THINKING	39-41
PROBLEM SOLVING	42-45
METACOGNITION	46-49

Strand: Decision Making (DM)		
Specific Outcomes for General Outcome: Identify the Problem		
K– Grade 4	**Grades 5-8**	**Gr. 9-12**
DM.A.1. Find the conflict or challenge in an issue.	DM.B.1. Define a conflict or challenge in an issue.	DM.C.1. Define a conflict or challenge in an issue and state reasons for it being a problem.
DM.A.2. Compile information that will be useful in responding to the challenge or conflict.	DM.B.2. Identify elements of a problem and relation among elements.	DM.C.2. Identify elements of a problem and relation among elements.
DM.A.3. State the problem in own words.	DM.B.3. State the problem in own words.	DM.A.3. State the problem in own words and justify reasons for the challenge or conflict.

Strand: Decision Making (DM)

**Specific Outcomes for the General Outcome:
Identify the Alternatives**

K– Grade 4	Grades 5-8	Grades 9-12
DM.A.4. Acknowledge that alternative views are possible.	DM.B.4. Consider alternative viewpoints and differences of opinions.	DM.C.4. Value the possibilities represented by alternative approaches.
DM.A.5. Recognize another point of view about an issue and give reasons for someone holding the view.	DM.B.5. Recognize a range of different interpretations of alternative approaches.	DM.C.5. Assess the relative merits of a range of viewpoints and come to own conclusions.
DM.A.6. Recognize that there might be misunderstandings on how other people view matters.	DM.B.6. Assess the relative merits of different interpretations and suggest why people may hold those views.	DM.C.6. Suggest ways by which conflicts of interest might be resolved to the benefit of most.

Strand: Decision Making (DM)

Specific Outcomes for General Outcome:
Evaluate Alternatives

K – Grade 4	Grades 5-8	Gr. 9-12
DM.A.7. Identify the steps to be followed to evaluate alternatives.	DM.B.7. Determine the criteria to be used for evaluating alternatives.	DM.C.7. Develop the ability to select and apply criteria of evaluation.
DM.A.8. Identify the strengths and weaknesses of alternative approaches.	DM.B.8. Identify the advantages and disadvantages of alternative approaches and justify choices.	DM.C.8. Identify the strengths and weaknesses of alternative approaches and justify choices.
DM.A.9. Assess the merits of alternative solutions.	DM.B.9. Identify the consequences of alternative actions.	DM.C.9. Identify the consequences of alternative actions and recognize solutions may have intended or unintended consequences.
DM.A.10. Identify actions or options to minimize problems.	DM.B.10. Discuss actions or options that can minimize a problem.	DM.C.10. Discuss actions or options that can minimize a problem.

Strand: Decision Making (DM)		
Specific Outcomes for General Outcome: Act on the Best Alternative		
K – Grade 4	**Grades 5-8**	**Grades 9-12**
DM.A.11. Recognize that action is required in making decisions.	DM.B.11. Recognize that decisions have to be acted upon.	DM.C.11. Recognize that action is required in the decision making process.
DM.A.12. Consider the possible consequences of actions.	DM.B.12. Consider the possible consequences of actions.	DM.C.12. Identify and list the possible consequences of actions based on own experiences.
DM.A.13. Recognize that some actions may affect other people.	DM.B.13. Recognize that some actions may impact other people's feelings and lives.	DM.C.13. Recognize that some actions may have an impact on other people's feelings and lives.
DM.A.14. Decide on what steps to follow and the means by which the solution may be put into effect.	DM.B.14. Decide on a course of action and the means by which it may be put into effect.	DM.C.14. Provide a rationale for a particular choice or action and provide a timeline.

Strand: Creative Thinking (C)		
Specific Outcomes for General Outcome: Exhibit Curiosity		
K – Grade 4	Grades 5-8	Grades 9-12
C.A.1. Show eagerness to pose questions that do not have straightforward answers. C.A.2. Speculate regarding possibilities. C.A.3. Demonstrate initiative and originality when developing ideas.	C.B.1. Seek out and identify new issues or problems to solve C.B.2. Pose thoughtful questions and probe for more information. C.B.3. Investigate alternatives	C.C.1. Ask questions for clarification. C.C.2. Keep a sense of purpose and direction in pursuing new problems. C.C.3. Recognize and tolerate ambiguity.

Strand: Creative Thinking (C)		
Specific Outcomes for General Outcome: Explore New Ideas		
Kindergarten – Grade 4	**Grades 5-8**	**Grades 9-12**
C.A.4. Contribute to brainstorming of ideas in pairs.

C.A.5. Contribute to discussion and explore new ideas.

C.A.6. Explore possible consequences of ideas. | C.B.4. Contribute to brainstorming of ideas in pairs and in groups.

C.B.5. Generate, build and combine ideas in new and flexible ways.

C.B.6. Deliberately pursue unusual and different solutions. | C.C.4. Contribute to brainstorming of ideas in pairs and in groups.

C.C.5. Make new associations between ideas and information.

C.C.6. Pursue personal insights, instincts and desires for new knowledge. |

Strand: Creative Thinking (C)

Specific Outcomes for General Outcome: Develop Flexibility

K – Grade 4	Grades 5-8	Grades 9-12
C.A.7. Be inquisitive and receptive to new ideas.	C.B.7. Be prepared to experiment and take risks.	C.C.7. Be prepared to experiment, take risks and consider another point of view.
C.A.8. Show openness to new ideas and methods and be able to see another point of view.	C.B.8. Respond to trying out and developing new ideas and seeing another point of view.	C.C.8. Recognize that risk taking can have setbacks.
C.A.9. Recognize that progress is not easy and difficulties may be experienced.	C.B.9. Persevere in the face of difficulty and setbacks.	C.C.9. Persevere in the face of difficulty and setbacks.
C.A.10. Recognize and accept that mistakes and setbacks are part of learning.	C.A.10. Recognize and accept that mistakes and setbacks are part of learning.	C.A.10. Recognize and accept that mistakes and setbacks are part of learning.

Specific Outcomes for General Outcome:
General Inquiry

K – Grade 4	Grades 5-8	Grades 9-12
CRIT.A.1. Distinguish between fact and opinions.	CRIT.B.1. Distinguish between facts and opinions.	CRIT.C.1. Distinguish between facts, opinions, preferences, and judgments.
CRIT.A.2. Draw inferences from the facts.	CRIT.A.2. Draw inferences from the facts and identify unstated assumptions.	CRIT.A.2. Draw inferences from the facts and identify unstated assumptions, stereotyping, and propaganda.
CRIT.A.3. Ask questions about the reliability of a source.	CRIT.A.3. Assess and pose questions about the reliability of a source.	CRIT.A.3. Assess and pose questions about the reliability of a source.
CRIT.A.4. Compare past and present sources.	CRIT.A.4. Identify ways of ensuring greater reliability by comparing past and present sources.	CRIT.A.4. Identify ways of ensuring greater reliability by comparing past and present sources.

Strand: Critical Thinking (CRIT)		
Specific Outcomes for General Outcome: Develop Inductive Reasoning		
Kindergarten – Grade 4	**Grades 5-8**	**Grades 9-12**
CRIT.A.5. Explore unfamiliar ideas or events and state observations.	CRIT.B.5. Explore the results of an observation or experiment.	CRIT.C.5. Explore and record the results of an observation or experiment.
CRIT.A.6. Examine patterns and regularities in observations and make generalizations.	CRIT.B.6. Analyze, observations and make generalizations from patterns and relationships.	CRIT.C.6. Analyze, evaluate observations and make generalizations from patterns and relationships.
CRIT.A.7. Recognize that some generalizations are not true.	CRIT.B.7. Recognize limitations of some inferences and generalizations.	CRIT.C.7. Draw inferences from these generalizations and recognize limitations.

Strand: Critical Thinking (CRIT)		
Specific Outcomes for General Outcome: Develop Deductive Reasoning		
Kindergarten – Grade 4	**Grades 5-8**	**Grades 9-12**
CRIT.A.8. Provide examples of a general law, which we know to be true, such as gravity. CRIT.A.9. Provide examples of a conditional statement. CRIT.A.10. Identify a rule and test it.	CRIT.B.8. Formulate a conditional statement about knowledge of topic. CRIT.B.9. Explain conclusions considered based on conditional statements given. CRIT.B.10. Confirm the premise and identify the general law.	CRIT.C.8. Formulate a conditional statement about knowledge of topic. CRIT.C.9. Identify the components of a conditional statement. CRIT.C.10. Confirm the premise and identify the general law.

Strand: Problem Solving (PS)		
Specific Outcomes for General Outcome: **Find and Define the Problem**		
Kindergarten – Grade 4	Grades 5-8	Grades 9-12
PS.A.1. Identify the problem in own words. PS.A.2. Identify problems that are created by our decisions and by Our behavior. PS.A.3. Identify problems that are created by forces outside of us. PS.A.4. Identify problems that can be solved in whole or in part.	PS.B.1. Identify and clarify the problem by asking questions. PS.B.2. Identify problems that are created by our decisions and behavior. PS.B.3. Identify problems that are created by forces outside of us and beyond our control. PS.B.4. Identify problems that can be solved in whole or in part.	PS.C.1. Identify, clarify, and paraphrase by asking probing questions. PS.C.2. Identify problems that are created by our decisions, behavior, and lack of experience. PS.C.3. Identify problems that are created by forces outside of us and beyond our control. PS.C.4. Identify problems that can be solved in whole or in part and discuss reasons for each solution.

Specific Outcomes for General Outcome:
General Possible Solutions

K-Grade 4	Grades 5-8	Grades 9-12
PS.A.5. Extract key words or points from a given source of information.	PS.B.5. Compare, contrast, and analyze a range of sources.	PS.C.5. Construct meaning by combining information acquired from a range of sources.
PS.A.6. Summarize information from a given source.	PS.B.6. Formulate questions to probe into the problem and to generate possibilities.	PS.C.6. Formulate probing questions to generate possibilities.
PS.A.7. Formulate questions to come up with possibilities.	PS.B.7. Formulate simple questions that are settled through definitions alone.	PS.C.7. Formulate simple and complex questions that are settled through definitions and argumentation.
PS.A.8. Determine if information addresses key questions.	PS.B.8. Determine if information addresses key questions and be able to defend choices.	PS.C.8. Assess the extent to which information addresses key questions and be able to defend choices.

Strand: Problem Solving (PS)		
Specific Outcome for General Outcome: Select and Implement a Plan		
K – Grade 4	**Grades 5-8**	**Grades 9-12**
PS.A.9. Discuss and brainstorm the steps of a plan. PS.A.10. Brainstorm the advantages and disadvantages of a plan. PS.A.11. Implement a plan and consider how choices are made.	PS.B.9. Identify the steps of a plan. PS.B.10. Examine the pros, cons and interesting points of a plan and use the process as a tool. PS.B.11. Implement a plan and establish a timeline.	PS.C.9. Identify the steps of a plan and determine a timeline. PS.C.10. Examine the pros, cons and interesting points of a plan and use the process as a tool. PS.C.11. Implement a plan and establish deadlines and timelines.

Strand: Problem Solving (PS)		
Specific Outcomes for General Outcome: Evaluate Results		
K – Grade 4	**Gr. 5-8**	**Grades 9-12**
PS.A.12. Review possibilities and determine if they make sense.	PS.B.12. Examine possibilities generated and eliminate unworkable ones.	PS.C.12. Examine possibilities generated and eliminate unworkable ones and give reasons.
PS.A.13. Describe patterns and relationships within information.	PS.B.13. Identify and evaluate some factors such as assumptions.	PS.C.13. Identify and evaluate factors such assumptions, stereotyping, propaganda.
PS.A.14. Explain how physical and emotional factors relate to produce patterns or relationships.	PS.B.14. Draw inferences and recognize flaws or weaknesses in analyzing information.	PS.B.14. Draw inferences and recognize flaws or weaknesses in analyzing information.
PS.A.15. Explain how some factors are connected.	PS.B.15. Explain how physical and emotional factors relate to produce patterns or relationships.	PS.C.15. Explain how physical and emotional factors relate to produce patterns or relationships.

Strand: Metacognition (M)		
Specific Outcomes for General Outcome: Develop Self Awareness		
K – Grade 4	**Grades 5-8**	**Grades 9-12**
M.A.1. Refine self awareness by talking about own family.	M.B.1. Refine self-awareness by doing self-assessment activities.	M.C.1. Refine self-awareness by group discussions and by taking self-assessment inventories.
M.A.2. Identify own interests, strengths and weaknesses.	M.B.2. Identify own interests, strengths and weaknesses.	M.C.2. Identify own interests, strengths and weaknesses.
M.A.3. Make personal goals and reflect on own performance.	M.B.3. Set personal goals, review progress and reflect on own performance.	M.C.3. Identify personal goals and establish timelines. Review progress and reflect on own performance.

Strand: Metacognition (M)		
Specific Outcomes for General Outcome: **Review and make Improvements**		
K – Grade 4	**Grades 5-8**	**Grades 9-12**
M.A.4. Take time to think before acting.	M.B.4. Take time to think before acting.	M.C.4. Take time to think before acting.
M.A.5. Review and discuss thinking, learning, and behavior.	M.B.5. Review and discuss thinking, learning and behavior.	M.C.5. Review and discuss thinking, learning, and behavior and relationships.
M.A.6. Brainstorm options and strategies for making improvements.	M.B.6. Identify and consider options and strategies for making improvements.	M.C.6. List and prioritize options and strategies for making improvements.

Strand: Metacognition (M)		
Specific Outcomes for General Outcome: Promote Time Management		
Kindergarten-Grade 4	**Grades 5-8**	**Grades 9-12**
M.B.7. Organize a sequence of activities.	M.B.7. Plan and organize a sequence of activities.	M.C.7. Plan and organize a sequence of activities and identify timelines.
M.A.8. Break tasks into sub-tasks.	M.B.8. Break tasks in sub-tasks and plan what to do next.	M.C.8. Break tasks into sub-tasks and prioritize the tasks.
M.A.9. Manage resources to meet deadlines.	M.B.9. Manage resources to meet deadlines.	M.C.9. Manage resources to meet deadlines.

48

Strand: Metacognition (M)

Specific Outcomes for General Outcome:
Refine Reflection Skills

K-Grade 4	Grades 5-8	Grades 9-12
M.A.10. Reflect on thinking and learning.	M.B.10. Reflect on thinking and learning.	M.C.10. Reflect on thinking and learning.
M.A.11. Learn to question own perspectives.	M.B.11. Learn to question own perspectives and motives and those of others.	M.C.11. Learn to question own perspectives and motives and those of others.
M.A.12. Monitor the use of new strategies to promote thinking.	M.B.12. Monitor the use of new strategies to promote thinking.	M.C.12. Monitor the use of new strategies to promote thinking and be able to justify choices.

ACHIEVEMENT INDICATORS

Along with General Learning Outcomes and Specific Learning Outcomes, Achievement Indicators correspond with the expected accomplishment for which they are used to measure performance. Achievement Indicators are sets of indicators that are used to determine whether students have met the corresponding specific outcomes. They are to supplement and expand the understanding of the specific outcomes. The purpose of the achievement indicators is to describe and demonstrate "what it looks like" when students are learning and completing the skills outlined within the content to reflect achievement levels (MECY, 2008b, p. 19).

Achievement indicators clarify for teachers, students, and parents what is expected of students, as they have descriptions of what students need to do in order to be considered competent and they correspond to the expected accomplishment for which they are used to measure performance on specific learning outcomes. They are also used to measure the extent to which expected accomplishments have been achieved and will make it easier for the teacher to know what to teach and make it easier to measure the attainment of the outcomes.

"Achievement indicators are one example of a representative list of the depth, breadth, and expectations for the outcome. Achievement indicators are pedagogy and context-free." (MECY, 2008b, p. 16)

ACHIEVEMENT INDICATORS AND GRADE LEVELS

The location and page numbers of the achievement indicators and grade levels are as follows:

STRANDS AND ACHIEVEMENT INDICATORS	Level A K-4 pages	Level B Grades 5-8 Pages	Level C Grades 9-12 Pages
DECISION MAKING	52-56	76-80	100-105
CREATIVE THINKING	57-60	81-84	106-109
CRITICAL THINKING	61-64	85-88	110-113
PROBLEM SOLVING	65-70	89-94	114-119
METACOGNITION	71-75	95-99	120-124

Strand: Decision Making (DM)   Grades K-4 – Level (A)
General Outcome: Identify the Problem
Achievement Indicators
The following set of indicators may be used to determine whether students have met the corresponding specific outcome.

DM.A.1. It is expected that the student will find the conflict or challenge in an issue:

- Define problem. What pertinent information is needed or missing?
- What part does dissatisfaction or contradiction play in a problem?
- State precisely or accurately what seems to be the problem?
- Recognize that a conflict or challenge may be different for other people.

DM.A.2. It is expected that the student will compile information that will be useful in responding to the challenge or conflict.

- Focus on available information and determine what you can learn from it.
- Formulate focused questions about a problem.
- Identify information that may be needed or missing.
- Take account of gaps in knowledge.

DM.A.3. It is expected that the student will state the problem in own words.
- What is the problem all about?
- Brainstorm the characteristics of a problem.

- Identify the elements of a problem and what makes it a problem.
- State the problem in a situation or issue in own words.

Strand: Decision Making (DM)   Grades K-4 – Level (A)
General Outcome: Identify Alternatives

DM.A.4. It is expected that the student will acknowledge that alternative views are possible.

- Listen to other people even when they have different viewpoints.
- Take time to discuss and consider alternative points of view and differences of opinion.
- Disagree respectfully by saying "I respectfully disagree…"

DM.A.5. It is expected that the student will recognize another point of view about an issue and give reasons for someone holding that view.

- Assess the relative merits of a range of viewpoints.
- Identify and discuss the pros and cons of alternative approaches.
- Suggest ways by which conflict of interest might be res `olved to the benefit of most.
- Explain why alternative approaches might be considered important.

DM.A.6. It is expected that the student will recognize that there might be misunderstandings on how other people view matters.

53

- Identify the difference between factual information and information based on biased opinion.
- Discuss different interpretations that may be attributed to biases depending on the culture, background, and worldviews of individuals.
- Explain why different points of views should be discussed.
- Identify reasons for misunderstanding or misinterpreting.

Strand: Decision Making (DM) Grades K-4 – Level (A)
General Outcome: Evaluate Alternatives

DM.A.7. It is expected that the student will identify the steps to be followed to evaluate alternatives.

- Brainstorm and discuss the advantages of certain actions.
- Brainstorm and discuss the disadvantages of certain actions.
- Consider how decisions affect other people.
- Consider how decisions may affect the future.

DM.A.8. It is expected that the student will identify the strengths and weaknesses of alternative approaches.

- Brainstorm ideas based on intuition, feelings, or hunches.
- Discuss how information influences interpretation of information.
- Find the positive and negative consequences of an alternative.

54

DM.A.9. It is expected that the student will assess the merits of alternative solutions.

- Brainstorm the elements of an effective decision.
- Discuss what determines the effectiveness of appropriateness of a decision. What are the needs and conditions to be satisfied?
- Discuss all the things in an alternative that might go wrong.
- Discuss all the positive aspects of a problem and their benefits.

DM.A.10. It is expected that the student will identify actions that can minimize a problem.

- Role play a problem by defending a position that is not your own.
- Suggest a compromise to achieve a win/win situation.
- Discuss empathy and role play different situations.

Strand: Decision Making (DM)   Grades K-4 – Level (A)
General Outcome: Act on the Best Alternative

DM.A.11. It is expected that the student will recognize that action is required in making a decision.

- Define decision as a resolution for future action.
- Distinguish between action and intention.
- Discuss the steps in a decision making process.
- Discuss how decision to take action was influenced.

- Discuss why compromise might be important.

DM.A.12. It is expected that the student will discuss the possible consequences of an action.

- Identify the possible consequences of an action.
- Discuss how decisions and actions affect other people.
- Discuss how decisions and actions may affect your future.
- Discuss the positive and negative aspects of the consequences.

DM.A.13. It is expected that the student will recognize that some decisions and actions may affect other people.

- Distinguish between intended and unintended consequences.
- How might your decision today affect the world?
- How might your decision today affect the future?

DM.A.14. It is expected that the student will decide on what steps to follow and the means by which it may be put into effect.

- Discuss why other people may have to know about your course of action.
- Discuss and outline how to notify other people of your decision to take action.
- Justify why this action or decision is the best choice at this time.

Strand: Creative Thinking (C)   Grades K-4 (A)
General Outcome: Exhibit Curiosity
Achievement Indicators
The following set of indicators may be used to determine whether students have met the corresponding specific outcome.

C.A.1. It is expected that the student will show eagerness to pose questions that do not have straightforward answers.

- Contribute to discussions
- Ask challenging questions during discussions
- Identify new problems to solve
- Show eagerness for discovery and wanting to know more

C.A.2. It is expected that the student will speculate on different possibilities.

- Make conjectures of possibilities
- Look for connections
- Ask more questions to explore issues
- Speculate on possibilities

C.A.3. It is expected that the student will demonstrate initiative and originality when developing ideas.

- Demonstrate initiative in developing ideas
- Create original ideas that no one has thought of.
- Follow through on ideas
- Search for more answers

Strand: Creative Thinking (C)   Grades K-4 – Level (A)
General Outcome: Explore New Ideas

C.A.4. It is expected that the student will contribute to brainstorming of ideas in pairs.

- Think of ideas to explore
- Feed imagination by inquiry.
- Create a list of ideas
- Examine questions that might help to develop more ideas.

C.A.5. It is expected that the student will contribute to the discussion and explore new ideas.

- Use imagination, generating own and different ideas.
- Elaborate on new ideas when questioned
- Listen to other people's ideas
- See the possible use of ideas
- Generate different possibilities.

C.A.6. It is expected that the student will explore possible consequences of ideas.

- Explore the possibilities
- Think through ideas, seeing where they may lead.
- Consider different scenarios
- Role play some scenarios.

Strand: Creative Thinking (C)   Grades K-4 – Level (A)
General Outcome: Develop Flexibility

58

C.A.7. It is expected that the student will be inquisitive and receptive to new ideas.

- Show willingness to take a chance and go beyond the obvious solution
- Consider other creative ways to generate ideas including visualization, mind maps, positive thinking strategies
- Show willingness to use drama, observation, interviews as ways of working

C.A.8. It is expected that the student will show openness to new ideas and methods and be able to see another point of view.

- Show openness to new ideas by being able to talk about different perspectives of the idea
- Show openness to new ideas and trying them out
- Display a positive attitude and have an open mind

C.A.9. It is expected that the student will recognize that progress is not always easy and difficulties may be experienced.

- Begin to accept that others may have different or conflicting
  points of view.
- Recognize that progress is not always easy.
- Recognize that others may not appreciate your work.

C.A.10. It is expected that the student will recognize and accept that mistakes and setbacks are part of learning.

- Identify the valuable learning experience that can come from mistakes.
- Appreciate that mistakes are a part of learning.
- Appreciate that being a risk taker is very difficult and takes courage.

Strand: Critical Thinking (CRIT)   Grades K-4 (A)
General Outcome: General Inquiry
Achievement Indicators
The following set of indicators may be used to determine whether students have met the corresponding specific outcome.

CRIT.A.1. It is expected that the student will distinguish between fact and opinion.

- State facts and opinions.
- Detect unsupported opinions.
- Detect bias in opinions.
- Consider the underlying rationale for each opinion

CRIT.A.2. It is expected that the student will draw inferences from the facts.

- Extract inferences from facts.
- What is stated and not stated in the information?
- What is being implied in the information?
- Determine the criteria for weighing evidence.

CRIT.A.3. It is expected that the student will ask questions about the reliability of a source.

- Define reliable evidence
- Ask questions about the dependability of data.
- Question how the information was obtained and it is useful.
- Apply informed skepticism in weighing evidence.

61

CRIT.A.4. It is expected that the student will compare past and present sources.

- Question if the evidence provides the information required.
- Question the consistency of data.
- Are your sources trustworthy?
- Research past and present sources of information.

Strand: Critical Thinking (CRIT) Grades K-4 (A)
General Outcome: Develop Inductive Thinking

CRIT.A.5. It is expected that the student will explore unfamiliar ideas or events and state observations.

- Discover and investigate unfamiliar ideas, events, or observations.
- Plan the steps of an observation or experiment.
- Record the results of an observation.

CRIT.A.6. It is expected that the student will examine patterns and regularities in an observation and make generalizations.

- Analyze observations and make generalizations from patterns.
- Formulate a guess or hypothesis that can be explored.
- Make a generalization based on limited number of observations i.e. this swan is white, therefore all swans are white.

62

- Recognize the flaws and weaknesses of inductive reasoning or generalizations without a valid or true conclusion.

CRIT.A.7. It is expected that the student will recognize these generalizations are not true.

- The validity of inductive reasoning is not dependent on the rules of formal logic.
- The evidence by all the premises is never conclusive.
- Draw inferences from these generalizations and recognize limitations.
- Examine some examples where discrimination is based on inductive reasoning. I.e. looking at one person from a race and assuming all people in that race are the same.

Strand: Critical Thinking (CRIT) Grades K-4 (A)
General Outcome: Develop Deductive Thinking

CRIT.A.8. It is expected that the student will provide examples of a general law which we know to be true, such as gravity.

- Take a general scientific law and apply to certain cases, assuming law is true.
- Provide examples of a general rule, which we know to be true. I.e. all turtles have shells, the animal in my bag is a turtle, and therefore the animal in my bag has a shell.
- Formulate a conditional statement about knowledge of topic.

63

CRIT.A.9. It is expected that the student will provide examples of a conditional statement.

- Identify the components of a conditional statement.
- Apply reasoning from general to the particular.
- Provide examples of premise. I.e. all dogs are mammals, all mammals have kidneys, and therefore, all dogs have kidneys.
- Form the combination of ideas into a complex whole.

CRIT.A.10. It is expected that the student will identify a rule or premise and test it.

- Confirm the premise and identify the general law.
- Identify a rule or premise and test it.
- Deductive reasoning is more concerned with testing and confirming the premise or hypothesis.
- recognize that if conclusion is both valid and true, then it is considered sound.

Strand: Problem Solving (PS) Grades K-4
General Outcome: Find and Define the Problem
Achievement Indicators
The following set of indicators may be used to determine whether students have met the corresponding specific outcome.

PS.A.1. It is expected that the student will identify the problem in own words.

- What constitutes a problem? What are characteristics of problems?
- Brainstorm some ideas and questions to be considered about a topic/issue.
- Create a list of questions that need to be answered in investigation.
- Identify the problem as accurately and precisely as you can.

PS.A.2. It is expected that the student will identify problems that are created by our decisions and by our behavior.

- Brainstorm some ideas and questions to be considered about a topic/issue.
- Suggest some questions to investigate, such as an image or an issue.
- Examine some problems that are created by our daily decisions.
- Examine some problems that are created by our behavior.

65

PS.A.3. It is expected that the student will identify problems that are created by forces outside of us.

- Suggest some questions to investigate
- Examine some problems that are created by forces outside of us.
- Examine acts of nature, pollution, global warming.

PS.A.4. It is expected that the student will identify problems that can be solved in whole or in part.

- Brainstorm some ideas and questions to be considered about a topic/issue.
- Examine some problems that can be solved in whole.
- Examine some problems that can be solved in part and not whole.

Strand: Problem Solving (PS) Grades K-4 (A)
General Outcome: Generate Possible Solutions

PS.A.5. It is expected that the student will extract key words or points from a given source of information.

- Extract key words from information and define them.
- Organize information into relevant groups
- Identify the basic meaning of the terms crucial to the question.
- Develop categories for information accessed

PS.A.6. It is expected that the student will summarize information from a given source.

- Formulate different types of questions.
- Formulate focused questions.
- State a question as clearly and precisely as possible.
- Summarize information from a given source.

PS.A.7.It is expected that the student will formulate questions to generate possible
solutions.

- Define simple questions.
- Identify examples of simple questions – compare meanings of same word.
- Use a dictionary or thesaurus to find definitions.

PS.A.8. It is expected that the student will determine if information addresses key questions.

- Determine if all information is known and find out what is missing.
- Determine if a question addresses the problem.
- Use supplementary inquiries to refine findings.

Strand: Problem Solving (PS) Grades K-4 (A)
General Outcome: Select and Implement a Plan

PS.A.9. It is expected that the student will discuss and brainstorm the steps of a plan.

- Compare the similarities of related plans.
- Compare the differences of related plans.
- Can a rule or policy by applied to the problem.

PS.A.10. It is expected that the student will brainstorm the advantages and disadvantages of a plan.

- Brainstorm and identify the advantages of a plan.
- Brainstorm and identify the disadvantages of a plan.
- Consider the positive and negative consequences of a plan.
- Consider beliefs and values in taking action.

PS.A.11. It is expected that the student will implement a plan and consider how it is made.

- Apply the course of action and consider the impact of the choice.
- Consider the effect of your choice on other people.
- Consider the impact of the choice on yourself, i.e., feeling good, guilty, remorse.
- Consider the way decision was made – was it pressure by peers, teacher, parents.
- Develop a record for monitoring and recording information.

Strand: Problem Solving (PS) Grades K-4 (A)
General Outcome: Evaluate Results

PS.A.12. It is expected that the student will review possibilities to determine if they make sense.

- Identify patterns and changes in patterns.
- Explain how factors can change at different rates over time.
- Use a timeline to examine how influences on development change as they grow older.

PS.A.13. It is expected that the student will describe patterns and relationships within the information.

- Evaluate how factors such as personal experiences, local community, family, interrelate to impact on managing change.
- Discuss the strength of family and cultural influences that impact on the mental growth of an individual.
- Explain the connection of the factors.

PS.A.14. It is expected that the student will recognize how physical and emotional factors relate to produce patterns or conclusions.

- Recognize that physical factors impact on how we manage changes.
- Recognize that emotional factors impact on how we make changes.
- Make connections between physical and emotional factors and how they relate to patterns or events.
- Explain the connections of the factors in daily decisions.

69

PS.A.15. It is expected that the student will explain how some factors are connected.

- Recognize that factors and personal experiences connect on we see what is real.
- Discuss the importance of family and how they impact on how we make changes.
- Identify the factors that are connected to making decisions and problem solving.

Strand: Metacognition (M)   Grades K-4
General Outcome: Develop Self-Awareness
Achievement Indicators

The following set of indicators may be used to determine whether students have met the corresponding specific outcome.

M.A.1. It is expected that the student will refine self-awareness by talking about own family.

- Be able to put thoughts into words – say what you think.
- Use show and tell to tell about oneself and family
- Use different tools to find out more about oneself
- Use self assessment activities to explore various strategies.
- Use group discussions to explore further strategies and to help inform some personal learning goal.
- Use group discussions to help inform some personal learning goal.

M.A.2. It is expected that the student will identify own interests, strengths, and weaknesses.

- Identify aspirations through discussion and sharing.
- Consider personal goals and targets that will enhance your strengths.
- Become aware as to where there is a lack of direction.
- Identify an area for improvement.

M.A.3. It is expected that the student will make personal goals and reflect on own performance.

- Review progress and recognize achievements.
- Identify an area for improvement.
- Recognize limitations.
- Become aware as to where there is a lack of direction.

Strand: Metacognition (M) Grades K-4 (A)
General Outcome: Review and Make Improvements

M.A.4. It is expected that the student will take time to think before acting on a decision.

- Avoid making quick decisions and snap judgments.
- Identify strategies and options for decision making.
- Become more aware of the link between thinking, feeling and behavior.
- Consider how behavior impacts on the learning process.

M.A.5. It is expected that the student will review and discuss thinking, learning, and behavior.

- Review and discuss thinking about how to learn.
- Independently evaluate approaches to thinking and learning.
- Choose favored methods.
- Analyze and apply feedback to achieve intentions.
- Recognize that behavior impacts thinking and learning.

M.A.6. It is expected that the student will brainstorm options and strategies for making improvements.

- Discuss how behavior impacts on the learning process.
- Use and understand emotional triggers to improve decision making.
- Consider how choices impact on you and others.
- Articulate the links between thinking, feeling and behavior.

Strand: Metacognition (M) Grades K-4 (A)
General Outcome: Promote Time Management

M.A.7. It is expected that the student will organize a sequence of activities.

- Follow a set of instructions and complete an activity within the
  stated timeframe.
- Prioritize tasks and activities.
- Consider that the amount of time allocated to activity is adequate.

M.A.8. It is expected that the student will break tasks into sub-tasks.

- Follow instructions.
- Independently plan and organize activities.
- Focus on task.

M.A.9. It is expected that the student will manage resources to meet deadlines.

73

- Identify necessary information for an activity.
- Identify resources need to complete a project or assignment.
- Perform the task and complete before the deadline.
- Review before submitting.

Strand: Metacognition (M) Grades K-4 (A)
General Outcome: Refine Reflection Skills

M.A.10. It is expected that the student will reflect on thinking and learning.

- Demonstrate understanding of the information.
- Use pictures, diagrams, and writing to represent information.
- Record and present information in a range of formats.
- Acknowledge and provide feedback about what was learned.

M.A.11. It is expected that the student will learn to question own perspectives.

- Select new approaches to the information.
- Think about what you are thinking and learning.
- Use criteria to show understanding of information.
- Reflect on new learning and if others' viewpoints have impact on perspectives.

M.A.12. It is expected that the student will monitor the use of new strategies to promote thinking.

- Explore the use of new strategies.
- Examine the consequences of new strategies.
- Consider actions that might aid in one's thinking and learning.
- Think about what you are thinking.

Strand: Decision Making (DM) Grades 5-8 (B)
General Outcome: Identify the Problem
Achievement Indicators
The following set of indicators may be used to determine whether students have met the corresponding specific outcome.

DM.B.1. It is expected that the student will define a conflict or challenge in an issue.

- Define problem.
- What part does dissatisfaction or contradiction play in a problem?
- What makes it a problem? State pertinent information that is needed or missing?
- State precisely or accurately what seems to be the problem.
- Recognize that other people might not see a problem, in what you might consider a problem or conflict.

DM.B.2. It is expected that the student will identify the elements of a problem and see the relation amongst them.

- Focus on available information and what you can learn from it.
- Formulate focused questions about a problem.
- Identify information that may be needed or missing.
- Take account of gaps in knowledge.

DM.B.3. It is expected that the student will state the problem in own words.

76

- What is the problem all about?
- Brainstorm the characteristics of a problem.
- Identify the elements of a problem and what makes it a problem.
- What pertinent information is needed or missing?
- State precisely or accurately what seems to be the problem.

Strand: Decision Making (DM) Grades 5-8 (B)
General Outcome: Identify Alternatives

DM.B.4. It is expected that the student will consider alternative viewpoints and differences of opinion.

- Listen to other people even when they have different viewpoints.
- Take time to discuss and consider alternative points of view and differences of opinion.
- Disagree respectfully by saying "I respectfully disagree..."

DM.B.5. It is expected that the student will recognize the range of different interpretations of alternative approaches.

- Assess the relative merits of a range of viewpoints.
- Identify and discuss the pros and cons of alternative approaches.
- Suggest ways by which conflict of interest might be resolved to the benefit of most.
- Explain why alternative approaches might be considered important.

77

DM.B.6. It is expected that the student will assess the relative merits of different interpretations and suggest why people hold those views.

- Identify the difference between factual information and information based on biased opinion.
- Discuss different interpretations that may be attributed to biases depending on the culture, background, and worldviews of individuals.
- Explain why different points of views should be discussed.
- Identify reasons for misunderstanding or misinterpreting.

Strand: Decision Making (DM) Grades 5-8 (B)
General Outcome: Evaluate Alternatives

DM.B.7. It is expected that the student will determine the criteria to be used for evaluating alternatives.

- Brainstorm and discuss the advantages of certain actions.
- Brainstorm and discuss the disadvantages of certain actions.
- Consider how decisions affect other people.
- Consider how decisions may affect the future.

DM.B.8. It is expected that the student will identify the advantages and disadvantages of alternative approaches and justify choices.

- Define fact, opinion, stereotyping, and propaganda.

78

- Find examples of fact, opinion, stereotyping, and propaganda in the news.
- Discuss how information influences interpretation of information.

DM.B.9. It is expected that the student will identify the consequences of alternative actions.

- Brainstorm the elements of an effective decision.
- Discuss what determines the effectiveness of appropriateness of a decision. What are the needs and conditions to be satisfied?
- Discuss all the things in an alternative that might go wrong.

DM.B.10. It is expected that the student will discuss actions or options that can minimize a problem.

- Role play a problem by defending a position that is not your own.
- Suggest a compromise to achieve a win/win situation.
- Discuss empathy and placing yourself in other people's shoes.
- Discuss all the positive solutions to the problem or issue.

Strand: Decision Making (DM) Grades 5-8 (B)
General Outcome: Act on the Best Alternative

DM.B.11. It is expected that the student will recognize that decisions need to be acted upon.

- Distinguish between action and intention.
- Discuss the steps in a decision making process.
- Discuss how decision to take action was influenced.
- Discuss why compromise might be important.

DM.B.12. It is expected that the student will discuss and list the possible consequences of actions.

- Identify the possible consequences of an action.
- Discuss how decisions and actions affect other people and your future.
- Discuss why something might not work.
- Discuss the value and benefits of a solution.

DM.B.13. It is expected that the student will recognize that some actions may impact other people's feelings.

- Distinguish between intended and unintended consequences.
- How might your decision today affect the world?
- How might your decision today affect the future?

DM.B.14. It is expected that the student will decide on a course of action and the means by which it will be put into action.

- Discuss why other people may have to know about your course of action.
- Discuss and outline how to notify other people of your decision to take action.
- Justify why this action or decision is the best choice at this time.

Strand: Creative Thinking (C)   Grades 5-8 (B)
General Outcome: Exhibit Curiosity
Achievement Indicators

The following set of indicators may be used to determine whether students have met the corresponding specific outcome.

C.B.1. It is expected that the student will seek out and identify new issues or problems
to solve.

- Contribute to discussions
- Ask challenging questions during discussions
- Identify new problems to solve
- Show eagerness for discovery and wanting to know more
- Look for connections in issues.

C.B.2. It is expected that the student will pose thoughtful questions and probe for more information.

- Make conjectures of possibilities
- Look for connections
- Ask more questions to explore issues
- Speculate on possibilities

C.B.3. It is expected that the student will investigate alternatives.

- Demonstrate initiative in developing ideas
- Create original ideas that no one has thought of.
- Speculate on possibilities.
- Identify alternatives to address issue

81

- Analyze some influences on an issue

Strand: Creative Thinking (C) Grades 5-8 (B)
General Outcome: Explore New Ideas

C.B.4. It is expected that the student will contribute to brainstorming of ideas in pairs and in groups.

- Think of ideas to explore
- Feed imagination by inquiry.
- Create a list of ideas
- Examine questions that might help to develop more ideas.

C.B.5. It is expected that the student will generate, build and combine ideas in new and flexible ways.

- Use imagination, generating own and different ideas.
- Elaborate on new ideas when questioned
- Listen to other people's ideas
- See the possible use of ideas
- Suggest likely outcome for ideas.

C.B.6. It is expected that the student will deliberately pursue unusual and different solutions.

- Explore the possibilities
- Consider different scenarios for different solutions.
- Role play some scenarios.
- Develop new or additional possibilities for moving forward.

82

Strand: Creative Thinking (C) Grades 5-8 (B)
General Outcome: Develop Flexibility

C.B.7. It is expected that the student will be prepared to experiment and take risks.

- Show willingness to take a chance and go beyond the obvious solution
- Consider other creative ways to generate ideas including visualization, mind maps, positive thinking strategies
- Show willingness to use drama, observation, and interviews.
- Show willingness to participate and/or make mistakes.

C.B.8. It is expected that the student will respond to trying out and developing new ideas and considering another point of view.

- Show openness to new ideas by being able to talk about different perspectives of the idea
- Show openness to new ideas and try them out
- Display a positive attitude and have an open mind
- Listen to other people and consider their point of view

C.B.9. It is expected that the student will persevere in the face of difficulty and setbacks.

- Use determination to succeed.
- Try out new ideas and reflect critically upon them.
- Stay on task even when it becomes difficult.

- Recognize that progress is not always easy.
- Recognize that others may not appreciate your work.

C.A.10. It is expected that the student will recognize and accept that mistakes and setbacks are part of learning.

- Identify the valuable learning experience that can come from mistakes.
- Appreciate that mistakes are a part of learning.
- Appreciate that being a risk taker is very difficult and takes courage.

Strand: Critical Thinking (CRIT)   Grades 5-8   (B)
General Outcome: General Inquiry
Achievement Indicators
The following set of indicators may be used to determine whether students have met the corresponding specific outcome.

CRIT.B.1. It is expected that the student will distinguish between fact and opinion.

- State facts and opinions.
- Detect unsupported opinions.
- Detect bias in opinions.
- Consider the underlying rationale for each opinion

CRIT.B.2. It is expected that the student will draw inferences from the facts and identify unstated assumptions.

- Extract inferences from facts.
- What is stated and not stated in the information?
- What is being implied in the information?
- Determine the criteria for weighing evidence.

CRIT.B.3. It is expected that the student will assess and pose questions about the reliability of a source.

- Define reliable evidence
- Ask questions about the dependability of data.
- Question how the information was obtained and it is useful.
- Apply informed skepticism in weighing evidence.

CRIT.B.4. It is expected that the student will identify ways of ensuring greater reliability by comparing past and present sources.

- Question if the evidence provides the information required.
- Question the consistency of data.
- Determine if your sources are trustworthy.
- Research past and present sources of information.

Strand: Critical Thinking (CRIT) Grades 5-8 (B)
General Outcome: Develop Inductive Reasoning

CRIT.B.5. It is expected that the student will explore the results of an observation or experiment.

- Explore unfamiliar ideas, events, or observations.
- Plan the steps of an observation or experiment.
- Record the results of an observation.

CRIT.B.6. It is expected that the student will analyze observations and make generalizations from patterns or relationships.

- Examine patterns and regularities in the observation.
- Formulate a guess or hypothesis that can be explored.
- Make a generalization based on limited number of observations i.e. this swan is white, therefore all swans are white.

- Recognize the flaws and weaknesses of inductive reasoning or generalizations without a valid or true conclusion.

CRIT.B.7. It is expected that the student will recognize limitations of some inferences and generalizations.

- The validity of inductive reasoning is not dependent on the rules of formal logic.
- The evidence by all the premises is never conclusive.
- Recognize these generalizations are probably not true.
- Examine some examples where discrimination is based on inductive reasoning. I.e. looking at one person from a race and assuming all people in that race are the same.

Strand: Critical Thinking (CRIT) Grades 5-8 (B)
General Outcome: Develop Deductive Reasoning

CRIT.B.8. It is expected that the student will formulate a conditional statement about knowledge of topic.

- Take a general scientific law and apply to certain cases, assuming law is true.
- Provide examples of a general rule, which we know to be true. I.e. all turtles have shells, the animal in my bag is a turtle, and therefore the animal in my bag has a shell.

CRIT.B.9. It is expected that the student will explain conclusions considered based on onditional statements given.

- Apply reasoning from general to the particular.
- Provide examples of premise. I.e. all dogs are mammals, all mammals have kidneys, and therefore, all dogs have kidneys.
- Form the combination of ideas into a complex whole.

CRIT.B.10. It is expected that the student will confirm the premise and identify the general law.

- Identify a rule or premise and test it.
- Deductive reasoning is more concerned with testing and confirming the premise or hypothesis.
- Recognize that if conclusion is both valid and true, then it is considered sound.

Strand: Problem Solving (PS)   Grades 5-8 (B)
General Outcome: Find and Define the Problem
Achievement Indicators
The following set of indicators may be used to determine whether students have met the corresponding specific outcome.

PS.B.1. It is expected that the student will identify and clarify a problem by asking questions.

- What constitutes a problem? What are characteristics of problems?
- Brainstorm some ideas and questions to be considered about a topic/issue.
- Create a list of questions that need to be answered in investigation.
- Identify the problem accurately and precisely.

PS.B.2. It is expected that the student will identify problems that are created by our decisions and behavior.

- Brainstorm some ideas and questions to be considered about a topic/issue.
- Suggest some questions to investigate such as an image or an issue.
- Examine some problems that are created by our daily decisions.
- Examine some problems that are created by our behavior.

PS.B.3. It is expected that the student will identify problems that are created by forces outside of us and beyond our control.

89

- Examine some problems that are created by forces outside of us such as pollution, global warming, and over population.
- Examine some problems that are beyond our control i.e. acts of nature.

PS.B.4. It is expected that the student will identify problems that can be solved in whole or in part.

- Brainstorm some ideas and questions to be considered about a topic/issue.
- Suggest some questions to investigate an image or an issue.
- Examine some problems that can be solved in whole.
- Examine some problems that can be solved in part but not in whole.

Strand: Problem Solving (PS) Grades 5-8 (B)
General Outcome: Generate Possible Solutions

PS.B.5. It is expected that the student will compare, contrast, and analyze a range of sources.

- Extract key words from information and define them.
- Organize information into relevant groups
- Identify the basic meaning of the terms crucial to the question.
- Develop categories for information accessed

PS.B.6. It is expected that the student will formulate questions to probe into the problem and to generate possibilities.

- Formulate different types of questions.
- Formulate focused questions.
- State a question as clearly and precisely as possible.
- Analyze concepts that are problematic.

PS.B.7. It is expected that the student will formulate simple questions that are settled through definition alone.

- Define simple and complex questions.
- Identify examples of simple and complex questions.
- Use a dictionary or thesaurus to find definitions.

PS.B.8. It is expected that the student will determine if information addresses the key questions and be able to defend choices.

- Find out if all the information is known in order to address the problem.
- Recognize that complex questions have no 'correct' or definitive answer.
- Use supplementary inquiries to refine findings.

Strand: Problem Solving (PS) Grades 5-8 (B)
General Outcome: Select and Implement a Plan

PS.B.9. It is expected that the student will identify the steps of a plan.

- Compare the similarities of related plans.
- Compare the differences of related plans.
- Can a rule or policy by applied to the problem.
- Examine related problems and determine if the same technique can be applied.

PS.B.10. It is expected that the student will look at pros, cons, and interesting points of a plan and use the process as a tool.

- Brainstorm and identify the pros of a plan.
- Brainstorm and identify the cons of a plan.
- Consider the interesting points of a plan.
- Consider beliefs and values in using the plan and taking action.

PS.B.11. It is expected that the student will implement a plan and establish a timeline.

- Apply the course of action and consider the impact of the choice.
- Consider the effect of your choice on other people.
- Consider the impact of the choice on yourself, i.e., feeling good, guilty, remorse.
- Consider the way decision was made – was it pressure by peers, teacher, parents.
- Develop a record for monitoring and recording information.

Strand: Problem Solving (PS) Grades 5-8 (B)
General Outcome: Evaluate Results

PS.B.12. It is expected that the student will examine possibilities generated and eliminate unworkable ones.

- Explore all the positive possible solutions and their benefits.
- Brainstorm all the negative aspects of a solution and point out what cannot be done.
- Eliminate unworkable solutions.

PS.B.13. It is expected that the student will identify and evaluate some factors such as assumptions.

- Evaluate how factors such as personal experiences, local community, family, interrelate to impact on managing change.
- Discuss the strength of family and cultural influences that impact on the mental growth of an individual.
- Explain the connection of the factors.

PS.B.14. It is expected that the student will draw inferences and recognize flaws or weaknesses in analyzing information.

- Recognize that physical factors impact on how we manage change.
- Recognize that emotional facts impact on how we manage change.
- Make connections between physical and emotional factors and how they relate to patterns or events.

93

- Explain the connections of the factors in daily decisions.

PS.B.15. It is expected that the student will explain physical and emotional factors relate to produce patterns or relationships.

- Identify patterns and changes in patterns.
- Explain how factors can change at different rates over time.
- Recognize and describe the patterns within information.

Strand Metacognition (M)   Grades 5-8 (B)
General Outcome: Develop Self-Awareness
Achievement Indicators
The following set of indicators may be used to determine whether students have met the corresponding specific outcome.

M.B.1. It is expected that the student will refine self-awareness by doing self-assessment activities.

- Express thoughts into words – say what you think.
- Write and talk about oneself and family.
- Use different tools to find out more about oneself
- Use self assessment activities to explore various strategies.
- Use group discussions to explore further strategies.
- Use group discussions to express a personal learning goals.

M.B.2. It is expected that the student will identify own interests, strengths, and weaknesses.

- Make list of own strengths and weaknesses.
- Identify aspirations through discussion and sharing.
- Become aware as to where there is a lack of direction.
- Identify an area for improvement.

M.B.3. It is expected that the student will set personal goals, review progress and reflect on own performance.

- Consider personal goals and targets that will enhance your strengths.

95

- Review progress and recognize achievements.
- Identify an area for improvement and make a timeline.
- Recognize limitations.
- Become aware as to where there is a lack of direction.
- Reflect and review progress on own performance.

Strand: Metacognition (M) Grades 5-8 (B)
General Outcome: Review and Make Improvements

M.B.4. It is expected that the student will take time to think before acting on a decision.

- Avoid making quick decisions and snap judgments.
- Identify strategies and options for decision making.
- Become more aware of the link between thinking, feeling and behavior.
- Consider how behavior impacts on the learning process.

M.B.5. It is expected that the student will review and discuss thinking, learning, and behavior.

- Review and discuss thinking about how to learn.
- Independently evaluate approaches to thinking and learning.
- Choose favored methods.
- Analyze and apply feedback to achieve intentions.
- Recognize that behavior impacts thinking and learning.

M.B.6. It is expected that the student will identify and consider options and strategies for making improvements.

- Discuss how behavior impacts on the learning process.
- Use and understand emotional triggers to improve decision making.
- Consider how choices impact on you and others.
- Articulate the links between thinking, feeling and behavior.

Strand: Metacognition (M) Grades 5-8 (B)
General Outcome: Promote Time Management

M.B.7. It is expected that the student will plan and organize a sequence of activities.

- Follow a set of instructions and complete an activity within the stated timeframe.
- Prioritize tasks and activities.
- Consider that the amount of time allocated to activity is adequate.

M.B.8. It is expected that the student will break tasks into sub-tasks and plan what to do next.

- Break one big task into sub-tasks
- Prioritize sub-tasks and develop timeline.
- Independently plan and organize activities.
- Focus on task.
- Write plans on what to do next.

M.B.9. It is expected that the student will manage resources to meet deadlines.

- Identify necessary information for an activity.
- Identify resources need to complete a project or assignment.
- Perform the task and complete before the deadline.
- Review before submitting.

Strand: Metacognition (M) Grades 5-8 (B)
General Outcome: Refine Reflection Skills

M.B.10. It is expected that the student will reflect on thinking and learning.

- Contribute your understanding of what occurred during the course of activity or learning.
- Use pictures, diagrams, and writing to represent information.
- Record and present information in a range of formats.
- Use criteria to show understanding of information.
- Reflect on your thinking and learning.

M.B.11. It is expected that the student will learn to question own perspectives and motives and those of others.

- Discuss expectations of others after an activity.
- Discuss and reflect on how problems may occur because of different expectations of other people.
- Select new approaches on how to question other people's motives.

- Reflect on new learning and how others' viewpoints have impact on perspectives.

M.B.12. It is expected that the student will monitor the use of new strategies to promote thinking.

- Explore the use of new strategies.
- Examine the consequences of new strategies.
- Consider actions that might aid in one's thinking and learning.
- Think about what you are thinking.

Strand: Decision Making (DM) Grades 9-12 (C)
General Outcome: Identify the Problem
Achievement Indicators
The following set of indicators may be used to determine whether students have met the corresponding specific outcome.

DM.C.1. It is expected that the student will define a conflict or challenge in an issue and state reasons for it being a problem.

- Define problem. What is the problem all about?
- What part does dissatisfaction or contradiction play in a problem?
- A problem is an issue or obstacle that makes it difficult to achieve a desired goal or purpose. It could be a dissatisfaction or a contradiction.
- State precisely or accurately what seems to be the problem.
- What might be a problem for some people, might not be a problem for all – be able to see other people's point of view.

DM.C.2. It is expected that the student will state the problem in own words and make judgments about the most likely explanations.

- Focus on available information and what you can learn from it.
- Formulate focused questions about a problem.
- Identify information that may be needed or missing.
- Take account of gaps in information.

- State the problem and why it is a problem based on your judgments.

DM.C.3. It is expected that the student will identify the elements of a problem and relation amongst them.

- Brainstorm the characteristics of a problem.
- Identify the elements of a problem and what makes it a problem.
- Identify the relation in the elements of a problem.

Strand: Decision Making (DM) Grades 9-12 (C)
General Outcome: Identify Alternatives

DM.C.4. It is expected that the student will value the possibilities represented by alternative approaches.

- Listen to other people even when they have different viewpoints.
- Take time to discuss and consider alternative points of view and differences of opinion.
- Show willingness to listen and not get mad when disagreeing.
- Disagree respectfully by saying "I respectfully disagree..."

DM.C.5. It is expected that the student will assess the relative merits of a range of viewpoints and come to own conclusion.

- Assess the relative merits of a range of viewpoints.
- Identify and discuss the pros and cons of alternative approaches.

101

- Suggest ways by which conflict of interest might be resolved to the benefit of most.
- Explain why alternative approaches might be considered important.

DM.C.6. It is expected that the student will suggest ways by which conflicts of interest might be resolved to the benefit of most.

- Identify the difference between factual information and information based on biased opinion.
- Discuss different interpretations that may be attributed to biases depending on the culture, background, and worldviews of individuals.
- Explain why different points of views should be discussed.
- Identify reasons for misunderstanding or misinterpreting.

Strand: Decision Making (DM) Grades 9-12 (C)
General Outcomes: Evaluate Alternatives

DM.C.7. It is expected that the student will develop the ability to select and apply criteria of evaluation.

- Brainstorm and discuss the advantages of certain actions.
- Brainstorm and discuss the disadvantages of certain actions.
- Consider how decisions affect other people.
- Consider how decisions may affect the future.

DM.C.8. It is expected that the student will identify the strengths and weaknesses of alternative approaches and justify choices.

- Define fact, opinion, stereotyping, and propaganda.
- Find examples of fact, opinion, stereotyping, and propaganda in the news.
- Discuss how information influences interpretation of information.

DM.C.9. It is expected that the student will identify the consequences of alternative actions and recognize solutions may have intended and unintended consequences.

- Brainstorm the elements of an effective decision.
- Discuss what determines the effectiveness of appropriateness of a decision. What are the needs and conditions to be satisfied?
- Discuss all the things that might go wrong in the alternative solutions.
- Discuss all the benefits and value of a solution and the consequences.

DM.C.10. It is expected that the student will discuss actions or options that can minimize a problem.

- Role play a problem by defending a position that is not your own.
- Suggest a compromise to achieve a win/win situation.
- Discuss empathy and placing yourself in other people's shoes.

Strand: Decision Making (DM) Grades 9-12 (C)
General Outcome: Act on the Best Alternative

DM.C.11. It is expected that the student will recognize that action is required in the decision making process.

- Distinguish between action and intention.
- Discuss the steps in a decision making process.
- Discuss how decision to take action was influenced.
- Discuss why compromise might be important.

DM.C.12. It is expected that the student will identify and list the possible consequences of actions based on own experiences.

- Identify the possible consequences of an action.
- Discuss how decisions and actions affect other people and your future.
- Discuss all the positive and negative aspects of intended actions.

DM.C.13. It is expected that the student will recognize that some decisions and actions may have an impact on other people's feelings.

- Distinguish between intended and unintended consequences.
- How might your decision today affect the world?
- How might your decision today affect the future?

DM.C.14. It is expected that the student will provide a rationale for a particular choice or action and provide a timeline.

- Discuss why other people may have to know about your course of action.
- Discuss and outline how to notify other people of your decision to take action.
- Justify why this action or decision is the best choice at this time.

Grades 9-12 (C) Strand: Creative Thinking (C)
General Outcome: Exhibit Curiosity
Achievement Indicators
The following set of indicators may be used to determine whether students have met the corresponding specific outcome.

C.C.1. It is expected that the student will ask questions for clarification.

- Show willingness to ask questions and identify new issues.
- Seek clarity and actively seek to deepen comprehension.
- Pose and respond to questions clearly.
- Listen to, build on, and challenge the ideas of others.
- Show eagerness for discovery and wanting to know more.
- Look for connections in issues.

C.C.2. It is expected that the student will keep a sense of purpose and direction in pursuing new problems.

- Maintain eye contact with speakers and listeners.
- Participate constructively in group activities.
- Identify problems and pose solutions collaboratively.
- Make conjectures of possibilities
- Speculate on possibilities

C.C.3. It is expected that the student will recognize and tolerate ambiguity.

- Recognize the complexity and lack of clarity around some issues.
- Accept complexities and ambiguities in some issues.
- Synthesize information to identify the complex issues.
- Analyze some influences on an issue.

Strand: Creative Thinking (C) Grades 9-12 (C)
General Outcome: Explore New Ideas

C.C.4. It is expected that the student will contribute to brainstorming of ideas individually, in pairs, and in groups.

- Contribute to brainstorming.
- Think of ideas to explore.
- Feed imagination by inquiry.
- Create a list of ideas for sharing.
- Examine questions that might help to develop more ideas.

C.C.5. It is expected that the student will make new associations between ideas and
information.

- Identify how ideas relate to information that has been gathered.
- Exercise individuality in linking own ideas to a bigger picture.
- Articulate how ideas can be a combination of other ideas.

107

- Recognize that other people might have the same ideas.
- Elaborate on new ideas when questioned
- Listen to other people's ideas.

C.C.6. It is expected that the student will pursue personal insights, instincts, and desires
for new knowledge.

- Articulate personal insights or instincts about an issue.
- Pursue the meaning of "gut feeling."
- Suggest likely outcomes of ideas.
- Synthesize own ideas and reflect on them in the context of wider issues.
- Consider different scenarios for different solutions.
- Role play some scenarios.

Strand: Creative Thinking (C) Grades 9-12 (C)
General Outcome: Develop Flexibility

C.C.7. It is expected that the student will be prepared to experiment, take risks and consider another point of view.

- Show willingness to take a chance and go beyond the obvious solution
- Consider other creative ways to generate ideas including visualization, mind maps, positive thinking strategies
- Show willingness to use drama, observation, interviews
- Show willingness to participate and/or make mistakes.

108

CRIT.C.4. It is expected that the student will identify ways of ensuring greater reliability by comparing past and present sources.

- Question if the evidence provides the information required.
- Question the consistency of data.
- Are your sources trustworthy?
- Research past and present sources of information.

Strand: Critical Thinking (CRIT) Grades 9-12 (C)
General Outcome: Develop Inductive Reasoning

CRIT.C.5. It is expected that the student will explore and record the results of an observation or experiment.

- Explore unfamiliar ideas, events, or observations.
- Plan the steps of an observation or experiment.
- Record the results of an observation.

CRIT.C.6. It is expected that the student will analyze and evaluate observations and   make generalizations from patterns or relationships.

- Examine patterns and regularities in the observation.
- Formulate a guess or hypothesis that can be explored.
- Make a generalization based on limited number of observations i.e. this swan is white, therefore all swans are white.

- Recognize the flaws and weaknesses of inductive reasoning or generalizations without a valid or true conclusion.

CRIT.C.7. It is expected that the student will draw inferences from these generalizations and recognize limitations.

- The validity of inductive reasoning is not dependent on the rules of formal logic.
- The evidence by all the premises is never conclusive.
- Recognize these generalizations are probably not true.
- Examine some examples where discrimination is based on inductive reasoning. I.e. looking at one person from a race and assuming all people in that race are the same.

Strand: Critical Thinking (CRIT) Grades 9-12 (C)
General Outcome: Develop Deductive Reasoning

CRIT.C.8. It is expected that the student will formulate a conditional statement about knowledge of topic.

- Take a general scientific law and apply to certain cases, assuming law is true.
- Provide examples of a general rule, which we know to be true. I.e. all turtles have shells, the animal in the box is a turtle, and therefore the animal in the box has a shell.

CRIT.C.9. It is expected that the student will identify the components of a conditional statement.

- Apply reasoning from general to the particular.
- Provide examples of premise. I.e. all dogs are mammals, all mammals have kidneys, and therefore, all dogs have kidneys.
- Form the combination of ideas into a complex whole.

CRIT.C.10. It is expected that the student will confirm the premise and identify the general law.

- Identify a rule or premise and test it.
- Deductive reasoning is more concerned with testing and confirming the premise or hypothesis.
- Recognize that if conclusion is both valid and true, then it is considered sound.

Strand: Problem Solving (PS)   Grades 9-12 (C)
General Outcome: Find and Define the Problem
Achievement Indicators
The following set of indicators may be used to determine whether students have met the corresponding specific outcome.

PS.C.1. It is expected that the student will identify, clarify, and paraphrase the problem by asking probing questions.

- What constitutes a problem? What are characteristics of problems?
- Brainstorm some ideas and questions to be considered about a topic/issue.
- Create a list of questions that need to be answered in investigation.
- Identify the problem as accurately and precisely as you can.

PS.C.2. It is expected that the student will identify problems that we have created by our decisions, behavior and lack of experience.

- Brainstorm some ideas and questions to be considered about a topic/issue.
- Suggest some questions to investigate such as an image or an issue.
- Examine some problems that are created by our daily decisions.
- Examine some problems that are created by our behavior.

114

PS.C.3. It is expected that the student will identify problems that are created by forces outside of us and beyond our control.

- Examine some problems that are created by forces outside of us such as global warming, pollution, over population, acts of nature.
- Examine some problems that are beyond our control i.e. diseases

PS.C.4. It is expected that the student will identify problems that can be solved in whole or in part and discuss reasons for each solution.

- Brainstorm some ideas and questions to be considered about a topic/issue.
- Examine some problems that can be solved in whole.
- Examine some problems that can be solved in part and give reason for not being solved in whole.

Strand: Problem Solving (PS) Grades 9-12 (C)
General Outcome: Generate Possible Solutions

PS.C.5. It is expected that the student will construct meaning by combining information
acquired from a range of sources.

- Extract key words from information and define them.
- Organize information into relevant groups
- Identify the basic meaning of the terms crucial to the question.

115

- Develop categories for information accessed

PS.C.6. It is expected that the student will formulate probing questions to generate possibilities.

- Formulate different types of questions.
- Formulate focused questions.
- State a question as clearly and precisely as possible.
- Analyze concepts that are problematic.

PS.C.7. It is expected that the student will formulate simple and complex questions that are settled through definition and argumentation.

- Define simple and complex questions.
- Identify examples of simple and complex questions.
- Use a dictionary or thesaurus to find definitions.

PS.C.8. It is expected that the student will assess the extent to which information addresses key questions and defend choices.

- Determine if all the information is known in order to address the problem.
- Defend choices.
- Recognize that complex questions have no 'correct' or definitive answer.
- Use supplementary inquiries to refine findings.

Strand: Problem Solving (PS) Grades 9-12 (C)
General Outcome: Select and Implement a Plan

PS.C.9. It is expected that the student will identify the steps of a plan and determine a timeline.

- Compare the similarities of related plans.
- Compare the differences of related plans.
- Can a rule or policy by applied to the problem.

PS.C.10. It is expected that the student will look at pros, cons and interesting points of a plan and use the process as a tool.

- Brainstorm and identify the pros of a plan.
- Brainstorm and identify the cons of a plan.
- Consider the interesting points and consequences of a plan.
- Consider beliefs and values in using the plans and taking action.

PS.C.11. It is expected that the student will implement a plan and establish, deadlines and timelines.

- Apply the course of action and consider the impact of the choice.
- Consider the effect of your choice on other people.
- Consider the impact of the choice on yourself, i.e., feeling good, guilty, remorse.
- Consider the way decision was made – was it pressure by peers, teacher, parents.
- Develop a record for monitoring and recording information.

117

Strand: Problem Solving (PS) Grades 9-12 (C)
General Outcome: Evaluate Results

PS.C.12. It is expected that the student will examine possibilities generated and eliminate unworkable ones and give reasons.

- Examine the positive possible solutions and their benefits.
- Brainstorm all the negative aspects of a solution and point out what cannot be done and give reasons.
- Eliminate unworkable solutions and explain why.

PS.C.13. It is expected that the student will identify and evaluate factors and challenge assumptions, stereotyping, and propaganda.

- Evaluate how factors such as personal experiences, local community, family, interrelate to impact on managing change.
- Discuss the strength of family and cultural influences that impact on the mental growth of an individual.
- Challenge assumptions, stereotyping, and propaganda.

PS.C.14. It is expected that the student will draw inferences and recognize flaws or weaknesses in analyzing information.

- Identify flaws or assumptions in analyzing information.

118

- Explain how factors can change at different rates over time.
- Use a timeline to examine how influences on development change as they grow older.

PS.C.15. It is expected that the student will explain physical and emotional factors that relate to produce patterns and relationships.

- Recognize that physical and emotional factors impact on how we manage change.
- Make connections between physical and emotional factors and how they relate to patterns or events.
- Explain the connections of the factors in daily decisions.

Strand: Metacognition (M) Grades 9-12 (C)
General Outcome: Develop Self-Awareness
Achievement Indicators
The following set of indicators may be used to determine whether students have met the corresponding specific outcome.

M.C.1. It is expected that the student will refine self-awareness by group discussions and taking self-assessment inventories.

- Express your thoughts into words – say what you think.
- Write and tell about oneself, family and extended family.
- Use different tools to find out more about oneself.
- Use self assessment activities to explore various strategies.
- Use group discussions to explore further strategies.
- Use group discussions to articulate a personal learning goal.

M.C.2. It is expected that the student will identify own interests, strengths, and weaknesses.

- Write down own strengths and weaknesses and share.
- Identify aspirations through discussion and sharing.
- Consider personal goals and targets that will enhance your strengths.
- Become aware as to where there is a lack of direction.

- Identify an area for improvement and make timeline.

M.C.3. It is expected that the student will identify personal goals, and establish timelines, review progress, and reflect on own performance.

- Review progress and recognize achievements.
- Identify an area for improvement and review progress according to timeline.
- Recognize limitations.
- Become aware as to where there is a lack of direction.
- Reflect and review progress on own performance.

Strand: Metacognition (M) Grades 9-12 (C)
General Outcome: Review and Make Improvements

M.C.4. It is expected that the student will take time to think before acting on a decision.

- Avoid making quick decisions and snap judgments.
- Identify strategies and options for decision making.
- Become more aware of the link between thinking, feeling and behavior.
- Consider how behavior impacts on the learning process.

M.C.5. It is expected that the student will review and discuss thinking, learning, behavior, and relationships.

- Review and discuss thinking about how to learn.

121

- Independently evaluate approaches to thinking and learning.
- Choose favored methods.
- Analyze and apply feedback to achieve intentions.
- Recognize that behavior impacts thinking and learning.

M.C.6. It is expected that the student will list and prioritize options and strategies for making improvements.

- Discuss how behavior impacts on the learning process.
- Use and understand emotional triggers to improve decision making.
- Consider how choices impact on you and others.
- Be able to articulate the links between thinking, feeling and behavior.

Strand: Metacognition (M) Grades 9-12 (C)
General Outcome: Promote Time Management

M.C.7. It is expected that the student will plan and organize a sequence of activities and identify timelines.

- Follow a set of instructions and complete an activity within the
  stated timeframe.
- Consider that the amount of time allocated to activity is adequate.

M.C.8. It is expected that the student will break tasks into sub-tasks and prioritize tasks.

122

- Break one big task into sub-tasks
- Prioritize sub-tasks and develop timeline.
- Independently plan and organize activities.
- Focus on task.
- Write plans on what to do next.

M.C.9. It is expected that the student will manage resources to meet deadlines.

- Identify necessary information for an activity.
- Identify resources need to complete a project or assignment.
- Perform the task and complete before the deadline.
- Review before submitting.

Strand: Metacognition (M)   Grades 9-12 (C)
General Outcome: Refine Reflection Skills

M.C.10. It is expected that the student will reflect on thinking and learning.

- Contribute your understanding of what occurred during the course of activity or learning.
- Use pictures, diagrams, and writing to represent information.
- Record and present information in a range of formats.
- Use criteria to show understanding of information.
- Reflect on your thinking and learning.

M.C.11. It is expected that the student will learn to question own perspectives and motives and those of others.

- Discuss expectations of others after an activity.
- Discuss and reflect on how problems may occur because of different expectations of other people.
- Select new approaches on how to question other people's motives.
- Reflect on new learning and how others' viewpoints have impact on perspectives.

M.C.12. It is expected that the student will monitor the use of new strategies to promote thinking and be able to justify choices.

- Explore the use of new strategies and record.
- Examine the consequences of new strategies and justify thoughts.
- Consider actions that might aid in one's thinking and learning.
- Think about what you are thinking.

ASSESSMENT STRATEGIES

Competence in thinking skills and processes includes decision making, creative thinking, critical thinking, problem solving, and metacognition. Teachers have to ensure that they provide students with opportunities to demonstrate these characteristics by choosing a variety of assessment strategies. Teachers have to bear in mind the interconnections between teaching, learning, and assessment. Real change in the classroom cannot be achieved without integrating instruction with assessment. Van de Walle and Folk (2005) believe that assessment and instruction should be indistinguishable (p. 70). As teachers assess, they are also providing opportunities for learning. The search for quality assessment tasks is also a search for quality learning tasks. Teachers have to use a variety of assessment strategies to assess and evaluate student progress.

Assessment should be done as a teaching tool to extend instruction. Assessment should be done before, during and following the instructional period. There is considerable overlap with the principles of assessment for learning and developing thinking pedagogy. "Assessing *for* learning" is a process of finding out where the learners are, where they have to go, and how best to get there (MECY, 2006, p. 65). The document indicates that "Assessment *as* learning" is to provide chances for students to monitor and reflect on their learning as they are learning. The document further points out that "Assessment *of* learning" is to inform the parents or guardians about the students' level of learning in relation to the curriculum.

125

This portion of the document summarizes some of the strategies teachers can use to assess how students process knowledge, and how well students learn. Elder and Paul (2006) declare that questioning skills are essential for productive thinking (p. 3). They claim that in order to be skilled at thinking, we have to be skilled at questioning. Questions generate more questions, and drive thinking forward. Questions have to be included as an indispensable part of assessment. A short description of the strategies is provided, as well as the value and information obtained from each strategy. The assessment strategies include observation; discussion, and structured interviews; journals and learning–log writing; performance of authentic tasks; investigations or projects; and self or peer assessment.

> *"Assessment should recognize differences among students'*
> *attitudes, such as motivation and appreciation. Students*
> *should be involved in the assessment and evaluation*
> *process."*
> *(MET, 1997, p. 59)*

Observation

Observation is the systematic observation of students as they process ideas. Observation is probably the most frequently practiced form of assessment. Systematic observation will provide rich and valuable information about a student's attitude toward thinking skills and processes, feelings as a learner, preferred learning approaches, areas of interest, work habits, and social development (MET, 1997, p.60).

Some observation tools that can be used for assessment are: anecdotal records, checklists, rating scales, time sampling or running records.

An anecdote is an account of an event in a child's day. The record of this event can be detailed or brief. These short reports describe, in a factual way, the incident, its context, and what was said or done by the participant. In most cases, anecdotes focus on very simple, everyday interactions among children, and materials in the environment. Ideally, the anecdotal record should be recorded as it unfolds or immediately after. However, anecdotal records usually have to be written later at the end of the day. Keeping brief notes on index cards or sticky notes carried in a pocket can be helpful. Jotting one-word reminders or short phrases on the cards about the event can provide a set of reminders when the anecdote is written.

Characteristics of Anecdotal Records:

- simple reports of behavior
- result of direct observation
- accurate and specific
- gives context of child's behavior
- records typical or unusual behaviors

"Make a habit of recording quick observational data. There are lots of options. A full class checklist with space for comments is one method. Another is to write anecdotal notes on address labels and stick them into binders."

Discussions and Structured Interviews

Discussions and structured interviews are opportunities for the teacher and the student to share ideas. They provide a context for the exploration of a student's reasoning as well as determining how well a student understands a skill. They can be used to reveal how well a student can explain solutions. Discussions and structured interviews can provide an opportunity for a student to justify thinking and reasoning. These assessment strategies are useful for revealing student strengths and preferences, and for discussing alternative strategies (MET, 1997, p. 61).

Classroom discussions offer a change of pace from the regular everyday lecture. They open the door for active student participation. Discussions encourage students to challenge one another, and the teacher can see whether the lesson was understood. Classroom discussions not only benefit the students but the teacher as well. The teacher can use the classroom discussion to see how many students understand the material that was presented and whether any further classroom time needs to be dedicated to reinforcing the material. Students are empowered to be responsible for the discussion, while the instructor provides context and learning outcomes for the discussion.

Structured interviews provide specific information on a student's construction of meaning. Structured interviews should be brief and conducted in a relaxed atmosphere. The teacher needs to be non-judgmental and avoid engaging in instruction. Structured interviews should be conducted periodically with every student. If time becomes

128

an issue, interviews may be limited to students for whom a clear picture of achievement has not been established. The interview script should be designed to provide appropriate space for recording student responses and teacher impressions. The recording sheet can be stored in the teacher's recording system, or placed in the student's assessment portfolio.

Techniques such as starting out with pairs of students talking together, followed by rotating these partners, followed by a full group discussion, are a means to begin to establish comfort levels for students who tend to remain quiet. Some students may have a difficult time engaging in discussion because of shyness. Organizers can be used to group ideas and show conclusions drawn. Flow charts can also be used. Approaches can include a list of points that are identified. Discussions may lead to writing journals or essays.

> "Important insights into student knowledge, skills, and values revealed during an informal discussion or conference should be recorded or dated."
>
> (MET, 1995, p. 60)

Journal and Learning-Log Writing

Journal and learning-log writing provides an opportunity to record thoughts, feelings, reflection, personal opinions, and even hopes and fears during an educational experience. They are a means of recording daily experiences and evolving insights that may aid in personal growth. Journal writing also promotes critical reflection,

129

whereby personal worldviews may be challenged or questioned.

Journal writing provides a safe place to explore new ideas, or clarify views. Daily writing represents an opportunity for students to produce pictures and written expressions of thoughts and feelings, to ask questions, and to comment on their learning experiences. This strategy for gathering assessment data is often left unstructured – the content and the format may be determined by the student and teacher (MET, 1997, p. 62).

Some teachers instruct their students to keep a learning log. It is similar to a writing journal, but it is used to get students to respond to specific questions that have been planned as an integral part of instruction. Questions may be asked, before, during or following instruction. The learning log is issued to give students an opportunity to communicate their reflections using graphics or their languages. A learning log entry can reveal feelings and attitudes about learning.

Noteworthy journal and learning-log entries can be photocopied and added to a teacher's recording system, or placed in the student's assessment portfolio.

"Journal writing allows a student to clarify thinking;
Journal writing allows a student time to reflect on learning;
Journal writing provides students with a safe forum for identifying strengths, weaknesses, and interests."

(MET, 1995. p. 61)

Performance and Authentic Tasks

This assessment strategy involves presenting students with designed or authentic tasks. Performance emphasizes different thinking processes. Students are expected to provide a thorough account of the strategies and the reasoning needed to complete a task (MET, 1997, p. 63).

For the evaluation to be fair, students require an explanation of expectations before they begin any task.

This assessment strategy involves the following:

- Students should be active participants, not passive selectors of the single right answer.
- Intended outcomes should be clearly identified and should guide the design of a performance task.
- Students should be expected to demonstrate mastery of those intended outcomes when responding to all facets of the task.
- Students must demonstrate their ability to apply their knowledge and skills to reality-based situations and scenarios.
- A clear, logical set of performance-based activities that students are expected to follow should be evident.
- A clearly presented set of criteria should be available to help judge the degree of proficiency in a student response.

Teachers may want to include conferences or interviews as part of this assessment process. Rubrics developed by the teachers or teachers and students may also be used.

Investigations and Projects

Project-based learning is an instructional model that involves students in investigations of compelling problems that culminate in authentic products. Project-based learning has gained a greater foothold in the classroom as researchers have documented what teachers have long understood about students. Students become more engaged in learning when they have a chance to dig into complex, challenging, and sometimes even messy problems that closely resemble real life.

Students' abilities to acquire new understanding are enhanced when they are connected to meaningful problem-solving activities, and when students are helped to understand why, when, and how those facts and skills are relevant, according to Kovalik and Olsen (2005, p. 1.13).

Project-based learning goes beyond generating student interest. Well-designed projects encourage active inquiry and higher-level thinking. Thinking investigations involve students in extended explorations of problems. An investigation may present students with situations that include thinking about and using ideas related to other subject areas. Investigations sometimes should grow out of interests shown or problems posed by the students. It may take students days or weeks to complete an investigation. The investigative work involved is intended to provide information about students' abilities to: apply and learn skills; identify and define a problem; make and carry out a plan; create and interpret strategies; collect and record necessary information; organize data and look for patterns; persist while looking for more information if needed; discuss, review, revise, and explain results (MET, 1995, p. 63).

Students should produce an adequate record of the stages of development, as well as results and conclusion of investigations. An outline of the scoring system, to be used for evaluating the processes used and the work produced, must be given to the students as they start the investigation. It is advisable that students be involved in evaluating their investigative work. The students' reports, photographs, charts, and audio or video tapes can be stored in the assessment portfolios.

> "Projects should include the student's account of the stages of development, results, and conclusions. It is worthwhile to have the students produce the scoring system and evaluate their own work."
> (MET, 1997, p. 64)

Peer Assessment or Self-Assessment

Peer assessment involves having students assess the performance of other students. This is often appropriate in assessing group work, and is particularly valuable if both product and process are assessed. In group work, a range of relevant skills are employed in the process of producing the group product. As well as the ability to work with others, these skills include self management and organizational skills, and communication skills. Peer assessment may also occur between partners working on a task.

Involving students in assessing their own performance can be an invaluable learning experience. Self-assessment invites students to reflect on their own efforts in using thinking processes, and on their own successes in understanding and applying concepts and procedures. Self-assessment promotes students' ability to reflect on their own efforts to use thinking processes and their own success in understanding and applying procedures. Students take ownership for their learning when they have opportunities to reflect on their own learning. It also helps them to become independent thinkers (MET, 1997, p. 65).

In self-assessment, students may inform the teacher

- how well they think they understand a piece of content

- what they believe or how they feel about some aspect of the content

- how well they perceive they are working in class or in their group

Self and peer assessment can be facilitated by use of a teacher or student prepared questionnaire, daily journal writing, and student or group conferences.

"Methods of self-assessment: Questionnaire, Open-ended questions, Mind maps, Drawings, Writing prompts, Attitude inventories."
(Van de Walle & Folk, 2005, p. 80)

Assessment Portfolios

A portfolio is a collection of student work, a showcase for a student's work, or a place where many types of assignments, projects, reports, and writing can be collected.

MET (1995) states that teachers and students who engage in developing portfolios for assessing progress and learning often establish general and assessment portfolios (p. 66).

General portfolios provide:

- evidence of knowledge and skill acquisition

- evidence of appropriate use of processes

- opportunities for the student to practice evaluation and selection of best examples of one's own performance and learning

- a permanent record of students' work

  Assessment portfolios provide

- graphic or written descriptions of problem solving, performance tasks, investigations, etc.

- photographs, video and audio compact discs, flip charts, from assigned or self-designed project work and presentation.

- excerpts from the student's journal and learning log.

135

- computer generated examples of developing technology skills and knowledge.

- student self-reports on what has been learned, on feelings about oneself as a learner, and on attitudes towards thinking processes.

SUMMARY

The Thinking Processes Curriculum Framework of Outcomes is designed to help educators in the process of change and transformation of education for 21st century learners. Students using a thinking curriculum will learn how to learn and be active participants in the learning process. Students will acquire thinking skills and processes for effective thinking, and develop habits of mind that will help them gain more control on their behaviors as thinkers and problem solvers. Changes to pedagogical assumptions or a shift of beliefs is central to transformation of education in today's society. These changes need to recognize that educators, students, and communities are all part of the learning process.

Current pedagogic approaches need to be revised to fit the needs of society. Educators need to recognize and acknowledge that they have a powerful influence in the classroom and on their students. Educators have to develop productive habits of mind in students in order to prepare them for an information-intensive, fast-changing society. Those productive habits of mind have to be overtly taught and reinforced. These needed changes will require time and money as educators will need professional development to overcome limitations and to see the benefits of a thinking curriculum.

Today's youth are growing up in a world that is faced with pressing global problems that will demand resourceful solutions. Students have to develop efficient practices and good attitudes, in order to function well in a society that is constantly changing. The future will demand that workers learn, unlearn, and relearn new skills, so students need to develop and display flexible thinking and openmindedness. The educational environment must be an atmosphere where students can discuss and reflect on thinking. A nurturing environment is a critical component if students are expected to reflect on their understanding or misunderstanding. The students' misinterpretation may be a result of their own experiences or lack of experiences. Their experiences from home and community will be recognized, acknowledged, and respected as important factors in the learning process. Learners of the 21st century have to be actively engaged today, so they can emerge as dynamic, resourceful thinkers.

A social constructivist paradigm supports understanding in a contextualized learning environment, where students are active participants in the learning process and are involved in interactions with other people. Acceptance of constructivist premises about knowledge and knowers implies a way of teaching that acknowledges learners as active knowers. A Thinking Processes Curriculum acknowledges that feelings, attitudes, beliefs and values are involved in teaching thinking. The transformation of education will be successful if the hearts and minds of students are actively engaged.

REFERENCES

Alberta Education. (2005). *Social studies kindergarten to grade 12*. Program rationale and philosophy. Edmonton, AB: Author.

Alberta Learning. (2004). *Focus on inquiry*. Edmonton, AB: Author.

British Columbia Ministry of Health. (1983). *Making decisions: an approach to prevention*. Vancouver, BC: Author.

Council for the Curriculum, Examinations and Assessment. (2007). *Northern Ireland curriculum: Thinking skills and personal capabilities progression maps at key stage 3*. Retrieved March 10, 2009, from http://www.nicurriculum.org.uk

De Bono, E. (1976). *Teaching thinking*. England, UK: European Services.

De Bono, E. (1983). *De bono's thinking course*. London, UK: The Pitman Press.

Elder, L., & Paul, R. (2006). *The miniature guide to the art of asking essential questions*. Dillon Beach, CA: Foundation for Critical Thinking.

Fullan, M. (2007). *The new meaning of educational change*. New York, NY: Teachers College Press.

Kite, A. (2000). *A guide to better thinking: Teacher's guide*. London, UK: GL Assessment.

139

Kovalik, S. J., & Olsen, K. D. (2005). *Exceeding expectations: A user's guide to implementing brain research in the classroom.* Covington, WA: Books for Educators.

Lowery, L. F. (1996). *Thinking and learning: Matching developmental stages with curriculum and instruction.* Kent, WA: Books for Educators.

Manitoba Education and Training. (1995). *Kindergarten to grade 4 mathematics: Manitoba curriculum framework of outcomes and grade 3 standards.* Winnipeg, MB: Author.

Manitoba Education and Training. (1996). *A thinking framework: Teaching thinking across the curriculum.* Winnipeg, MB: Author.

Manitoba Education and Training. (1997). *Senior 1 math: Manitoba curriculum framework of outcomes and senior 1 standards.* Winnipeg, MB: Author.

Manitoba Education, Citizenship and Youth. (2003). *Kindergarten to Grade 8 Social Studies: Manitoba curriculum framework of outcomes.* Winnipeg, MB: Author.

Manitoba Education, Citizenship and Youth. (2006). *Rethinking classroom assessment with purpose in mind: Assessment for learning, assessment as learning, assessment of learning.* Winnipeg, MB: Author.

Manitoba Education, Citizenship and Youth. (2008a). *Communicating student learning: Guidelines for schools.* Winnipeg, MB: Author.

Manitoba Education, Citizenship and Youth. (2008b). *Kindergarten to grade 8 mathematics: Manitoba curriculum framework of outcomes.* Winnipeg, MB: Author.

Marzano, R. J. & Arredondo, D. E. (1986). Restructuring schools through the teaching of thinking skills. *Educational Leadership. 43*(8), 20-26.

Martin, K. L. (2003). Ways of knowing, ways of being and ways of doing: A theoretical framework and methods for indigenous re-search and indigenist research. *Journal of Australian Studies. 27(*76), 203-214.

McGregor, D. (2007). *Developing thinking, developing learning: A guide to thinking skills in education.* New York, NY: McGraw-Hill.

McGuinness, C. (1999) *From Thinking Skills to Thinking Classrooms: A review and evaluation of approaches for developing pupils' thinking.* London: DFEE Research Report RR115.

Ornstein, A., & Hunkins, F. (2004). *Curriculum foundations, principles, and issues.* Boston, MA: Pearson Education.

Saskatchewan Education. (1987). *Critical and creative thinking.* Retrieved March 9, 2009, from http://www.sasked.gov.sk.ca/docs/policy/cels/e14.html

Thayer-Bacon, B. J. (2000). *Transforming critical thinking: Thinking constructively.* New York, NY: Teachers College Press.

Toffler, A. (1990). *Powershift: Knowledge, wealth, and violence at the edge of the 21st century.* New York, NY: Bantam Books.

Van de Walle, J. A., & Folk, S. (2005). *Elementary and middle school mathematics: Teaching developmentally.* Toronto, ON: Pearson Education.

Van de Walle, J. A., & Lovin, L. H. (2006). *Teaching student-centered mathematics: Grades k-3.* Boston, MA: Pearson Education.

Victorian Curriculum and Assessment Authority. (2008). *Victorian Essential Learning Standards.* Victoria, AU: Author.

Walker, C., & Antaya-Moore, D. (1999). *Thinking tools for kids: Practical organizers.* Edmonton, AB: Edmonton Public Schools.

Walsh, G., Murphy, P., & Dunbar, C. (2007). *Thinking skills in the early years: A guide for practitioners.* Belfast, UK: Stranmillis University College.

Wiles, J., & Bondi, J. (2007). *Curriculum development: A guide to practice.* Upper Saddle River, NJ: Pearson Education.

Wilks, S. (2005). *Designing a thinking curriculum.* Victoria, AU: Australian Council for Educational Research.

Wilson, S. (2001). What is an indigenous research methodology? *Canadian Journal of Native Education, 25*(2), 175-179.

Wilson, S. (2008). *Research is ceremony: Indigenous research methods*. Winnipeg, MB: Fernwood.

RECOMMENDED RESOURCES

Overview of the more common commercial packages for developing thinking

The following list is a selection from hundreds of resources; therefore it is not an exhaustive list.

Adey, P., & Shayer, M., & Yeates, C. (1981). *Cognitive acceleration through science education.* Retrieved January 23, 2010, from http://www.nelsonthornes.com/secondary/science/books_thinking.htm

De Bono, E. (n.d.). *Effective thinking: a general thinking skills course.* Retrieved November 30, 2009, from http://www.edwdebono.com/course/index.htm

De Bono, E. (1970). *Lateral thinking.* London: Penguin.

De Bono, E. (1985). *Six thinking hats.* London: Penguin.

Blagg, N., & Ballinger, M. (1989). *The somerset thinking skills.* Retrieved January 23, 2010 from http://www.somersetthinkingskills.co.uk/modules.html

Smith, A. & Call, N. (1999). *The ALPS approach: Accelerated learning in primary schools.* Brain-based methods for accelerating motivation and achievement. Stafford: Network Educational Press.

SAMPLE LESSON PLAN

The philosophy recommended is pragmatism.

Pragmatism construes knowledge as a process in which reality is constantly changing. Knowing is a transaction between the learner and the environment, so both learner and environment are constantly changing, as are the transactions or experiences.

Social constructivism is a theory of learning. In social constructivism, the central notion of thinking and understanding originates through social interactions, which then form personal constructions of meaning. The learner connects new learning with already existing knowledge based on personal experiences. Our ideas and perceptions come from our experiences and transactions with each other.

Teaching is more exploratory than explanatory. Encourage reflective thought and action. Students learn most effectively when they develop the ability to stand back from the information or ideas that they have engaged with and think about these objectively. Reflective thinkers assimilate new learning, relate it to what they know already, and come to change their ways of perceiving something. Learning is inseparable from its social and cultural context. Students learn best when they feel accepted, when they enjoy positive relationships with their fellow students and teachers, and when they are able to be active members of the learning community.

The lesson plan has a before, during, and after part of the lesson. The **before** part involves the activating of learning,

145

the **during** part involves the acquiring of learning, and the **after** part involves the application of the learning.

In this lesson, students have to answer a question based on a movie that they have watched. "What is the main problem in the movie "Avatar"?

In a previous lesson, a problem was defined as **an issue or obstacle that makes it difficult to achieve a desired goal or purpose. It could be a dissatisfaction or a contradiction.**

Strand   **__DECISION   MAKING_____**
Level - C_____ **Grades 9-12** _____

General Learning Outcome	Specific Learning Outcome	Achievement Indicator(s)
Identify the problem	Define a conflict or challenge in an issue and state the reasons for it being a problem.	What might be a problem for some people might not be a problem for all- be able to see other people's point of view.

TEACHING AND LEARNING ACTIVITIES	ASSESSMENT

146

BEFORE	Assessment for Learning:
Inform students that they have to answer a question on a movie that they have seen. They will record their ideas in their journals when they work in pairs for the first 10 minutes. Ideas from students are not judged, just documented. Then they will work in groups and have a discussion of their ideas and perceptions. Listen to other people's ideas and look them in the eyes as they speak. At the end of class, the students will record in their journals again on what ideas or perceptions have changed. **Question:** What is the main problem in the movie "Avatar?"	Keep accurate and up-to-date anecdotes and interpretations. Provide clear, detailed learning expectations by giving a rubric that indicates: Excellent, Satisfactory and Needs Improvement. Provide each student with a journal so the teacher can provide feedback on student's understanding or misunderstanding and also to further student's learning. A view of the journals will indicate if their views have changed in the process of listening to other people. Do they still hold the views that they had at the start of the lesson?

DURING	Assessment as Learning:
When they start working in groups, there should be	Guide and provide opportunities for each student

a recorder, and someone designated to present the information later on.	to monitor and critically reflect on his/her learning and identify each step.
The recorder will record the brainstorming of what they think is the problem (or problems) in the movie "Avatar."	Students record their own perceptions in their journals.
The students will listen to each other as they interpret what they think is the problem and why.	Provide students with ideas for adjusting, rethinking, and articulating learning. Students to do self-reflection, self-monitoring, and self-adjustment.
The students will share with the larger group and find out what other people have discussed.	Are students comfortable with the amount of time given to the discussion of their perceptions?
Think of different perspectives on the issue(s).	
What is the problem according to the Indigenous people? Put yourself in their shoes and imagine why they hold their views.	
What is the problem according to the people looking for the mineral? Put yourself in their shoes and imagine why they might hold their views.	

AFTER	Assessment of Learning:
Reflect on the learning of the students. Were you able to see other people's point of view? Did you try to make other people realize your view was right or did you show respect and listen to their point of view. Was it hard to accept that other people have different interpretations? By looking at various perspectives, students develop empathy for the experiences, feelings, and worldviews of other people. **EXIT CARD ACTIVITY:** Write 2 questions about this activity and write one comment.	Report fair, accurate, and detailed information that can be used to decide the next steps in a student's learning. Did you provide clear, detailed learning expectations. Can you tell the extent to which students can apply the skills, and attitudes related to the thinking curriculum? Inform parents of students' proficiency in relation to learning outcomes.
RESOURCES Journals for ideas. Flipchart paper and markers for the recorders in the groups. Tables for discussion groups. Exit card activity.	

CPSIA information can be obtained at www.ICGtesting.com
Printed in the USA
LVOW12s1925061214

417553LV00002B/466/P